Company's Coming

School Days Parties

Jean Paré

companyscoming.com
visit our ↑ website

Front Cover

1. Sparkling Raspberry Punch, page 16
2. Chocolate Microphones, page 19
3. Shortbread Stars, page 18
4. Chicken Satay Skewers, page 17
5. Ham And Cheese Pinwheels, page 16

Back Cover

Cookie Bouquets, page 84

First Printing July 2004

National Library of Canada Cataloguing in Publication

Paré, Jean
        School days parties / Jean Paré.

(Original series)
Includes index.
ISBN 1-896891-82-9

        1. Children's parties. 2. Cookery. I. Title. II. Series.

TX731.P374 2004   641.5'68   C2003-905239-7

Published by
COMPANY'S COMING PUBLISHING LIMITED
2311 – 96 Street
Edmonton, Alberta, Canada T6N 1G3
Tel: (780) 450-6223   Fax: (780) 450-1857
www. companyscoming.com

Company's Coming is a registered trademark owned by Company's Coming Publishing Limited

Printed in China

We gratefully acknowledge the following suppliers for their generous support of our Test Kitchen and Photo Studio:

Broil King Barbecues   *Lagostina ®*
Corelle ®   *Proctor Silex ®*
Hamilton Beach ®   *Canada*
*   Canada*   *Tupperware ®*

Our special thanks to the following businesses for providing extensive props for photography:

Anchor Hocking   *Klass Works*
*   Canada*   *Michaels The Arts*
Brown & Co. Ltd.   *And Crafts Store*
Canadian Tire   *Partyland*
Canhome Global   *Pfaltzgraff Canada*
Casa Bugatti   *Pier 1 Imports*
Cherison Enterprises   *Sears Canada*
*   Inc.*   *Stokes*
Corelle®   *The Bay*
Danesco Inc.   *Walmart Canada*
Dansk Gifts   *   Inc.*
Island Pottery Inc.   *Winners Stores*
Kitchen Treasures   *Zellers*

Visit us on-line

companyscoming.com

| Who We Are | Browse Cookbooks | Cooking Tonight? | Home |

everyday ingredients

feature recipes

feature recipes

tips and tricks

reader circle

cooking links

cookbook search

contact us

Cooking tonight? Check out this month's ***feature recipes***—absolutely FREE!

Looking for some great kitchen helpers? ***tips and tricks*** are here to save the day!

In search of answers to cooking or household questions? Do you have answers you'd like to share? Join the fun with ***reader circle***, our on-line question and answer bulletin board. Great for swapping recipes too!

Other interesting and informative web-sites are just a click away with ***cooking links.***

Find cookbooks by title, description or food category using ***cookbook search***.

We want to hear from you—***contact us*** lets you offer suggestions for upcoming titles, or share your favourite recipes.

Company's Coming
COOKBOOKS

Canada's
**most popular
cookbooks!**

Company's Coming Cookbook Series

Original Series

- Softcover, 160 pages
- 6" x 9" (15 cm x 23 cm) format
- Lay-flat binding
- Full colour photos
- Nutrition information

Quick & easy recipes, everyday ingredients!

Greatest Hits Series

- Softcover, 106 & 124 pages
- 8" x 9 9/16" (20 cm x 24 cm) format
- Paperback binding
- Full colour photos
- Nutrition information

Lifestyle Series

- Softcover, 160 pages
- 8" x 10" (20 cm x 25 cm) format
- Paperback & spiral binding
- Full colour photos
- Nutrition information

Most Loved Recipe Collection

- Hardcover, 128 pages
- 8 3/4" x 8 3/4" (22 cm x 22 cm) format
- Full colour throughout
- Nutrition information

Special Occasion Series

- Hardcover & softcover, 192 pages
- 8 1/2" x 11" (22 cm x 28 cm) format
- Durable sewn binding
- Full colour throughout
- Nutrition information

See page 157 for a complete listing of <u>all</u> cookbooks or visit companyscoming.com

Table of Contents

The Company's Coming Story

Jean Paré grew up understanding that the combination of family, friends and home cooking is the essence of a good life. From her mother she learned to appreciate good cooking, while her father praised even her earliest attempts. When she left home she took with her many acquired family recipes, a love of cooking and an intriguing desire to read recipe books like novels!

"never share a recipe you wouldn't use yourself"

In 1963, when her four children had all reached school age, Jean volunteered to cater the 50th anniversary of the Vermilion School of Agriculture, now Lakeland College. Working out of her home, Jean prepared a dinner for over 1000 people which launched a flourishing catering operation that continued for over eighteen years. During that time she was provided with countless opportunities to test new ideas with immediate feedback— resulting in empty plates and contented customers! Whether preparing cocktail sandwiches for a house party or serving a hot meal for 1500 people, Jean Paré earned a reputation for good food, courteous service and reasonable prices.

"Why don't you write a cookbook?" Time and again, as requests for her recipes mounted, Jean was asked that question. Jean's response was to team up with her son, Grant Lovig, in the fall of 1980 to form Company's Coming Publishing Limited. April 14, 1981 marked the debut of "150 DELICIOUS SQUARES," the first Company's Coming cookbook in what soon would become Canada's most popular cookbook series.

Jean Paré's operation has grown steadily from the early days of working out of a spare bedroom in her home. Full-time staff includes marketing personnel located in major cities across Canada. Home Office is based in Edmonton, Alberta in a modern building constructed specially for the company.

Today the company distributes throughout Canada and the United States in addition to numerous overseas markets, all under the guidance of Jean's daughter, Gail Lovig. Best-sellers many times over in English, Company's Coming cookbooks have also been published in French and Spanish. Familiar and trusted in home kitchens around the world, Company's Coming cookbooks are offered in a variety of formats, including the original softcover series.

Jean Paré's approach to cooking has always called for quick and easy recipes using everyday ingredients. Even when travelling, she is constantly on the lookout for new ideas to share with her readers. At home, she can usually be found researching and writing recipes, or working in the company's test kitchen. Jean continues to gain new supporters by adhering to what she calls "the golden rule of cooking:" never share a recipe you wouldn't use yourself. It's an approach that works—*millions of times over*!

Foreword

The school year is a very busy time for parents and students alike, but there are plenty of opportunities to celebrate and have fun with your kids. In *School Days Parties*, we offer ideas and creative menu plans for those events that fall within the school year, such as Halloween and Spring Break. There are menus for birthday parties, such as the Medieval Party or Dinosaur Dig. Use these menus at any time of year, whether you have something to celebrate or just need a break from the usual routine. With *School Days Parties*, it's easy to create delicious, attractive food that kids will love.

Because you don't have a lot of time in a hectic household, we've ensured most of our recipes are quick and easy to prepare. School Days Parties simplifies food preparation by using common, everyday ingredients in fun, unique recipes.

All great parties begin with good planning. We've made it easy for you to put together a well-organized party by dividing this book into twenty themed menus. Prepare all of the items in a menu, or pick and choose from various menus, depending on the party and your child's tastes.

School Days Parties is a kid-friendly book. Although the recipes are written for adults to prepare, colour pictures accompany each menu. Let your child flip through the pictures and pick the foods they would like to have at their party. Depending on the age of the children, encourage them to assist you for the day and help with food preparation and decorations. Get the whole family involved, if possible, and enjoy the party day together.

School years are filled with great memories, but a child's time can be quickly consumed by too many activities. *School Days Parties* will remind you to slow down and take time for fun throughout the school year. Enjoy your children every step of the way and celebrate at every turn with family, friends, fun and great food!

Jean Paré

Each recipe has been analyzed using the most up-to-date version of the Canadian Nutrient File from Health Canada, which is based on the United States Department of Agriculture (USDA) Nutrient Database. If more than one ingredient is listed (such as "hard margarine or butter"), then the first ingredient is used in the analysis. Where an ingredient reads "sprinkle," "optional," or "for garnish," it is not included as part of the nutrition information.

Margaret Ng, B.Sc. (Hon), M.A.
Registered Dietitian

Dinosaur Dig

Stomp with the dinosaurs to celebrate prehistoric times with a birthday party your kids will never forget. Boys and girls alike will enjoy these unique recipes.

serves 8

Frothy Lime Punch

Guess-The-Dinosaur Toast

Ancient Animal Bones

Prehistoric Fish Scales

Dinosaur Cake

Top Left: Prehistoric Fish Scales, page 11
Top Centre and Bottom Right: Frothy Lime Punch, page 10
Top Right: Ancient Animal Bones, page 11
Bottom Left: Guess-The-Dinosaur Toast, page 10

Frothy Lime Punch

A bright green, refreshing drink topped with white froth.

Pineapple juice	4 cups	1 L
Envelope of unsweetened lime-flavoured drink mix (such as Kool-Aid)	1/4 oz.	6 g
Granulated sugar	1 cup	250 mL
Lime sherbet	2 cups	500 mL
Ginger ale	4 cups	1 L
Lime slices	8	8

Stir pineapple juice, drink mix and sugar in large pitcher until sugar is dissolved.

Spoon about 1/4 cup (60 mL) sherbet into each of eight 10 to 12 oz. (284 to 341 mL) glasses. Add about 1/2 cup (125 mL) pineapple mixture to each glass.

Slowly add about 1/2 cup (125 mL) ginger ale to each glass so froth forms on top.

Cut lime slices just to centre. Place 1 slice on edge of each glass. Serves 8.

1 serving: 290 Calories; 1.1 g Total Fat (0.3 g Mono, 0.1 g Poly, 0.6 g Sat); 3 mg Cholesterol; 71 g Carbohydrate; trace Fibre; 1 g Protein; 34 mg Sodium

Pictured on page 9.

Guess-The-Dinosaur Toast

Cute dinosaurs in fun colours. Ask the baker a day or two ahead to cut a loaf into lengthwise slices.

Hard margarine, softened	1/3 cup	75 mL
Garlic powder, sprinkle		
Onion powder, sprinkle		
Liquid (or paste) food colouring, your child's choice (see Note)		
Day-old white (or brown) sandwich loaf, cut lengthwise into 1/2 inch (12 mm) thick slices and crusts removed	1	1

Combine margarine, garlic powder and onion powder in small dish. Remove 2 1/2 tbsp. (37 mL) to separate small dish. Add different food colouring to each dish.

(continued on next page)

Spread margarine mixture thinly on 1 side of each bread slice, alternating colours. Cut dinosaur shapes from bread slices with cookie cutters. Arrange, buttered side up, in single layer on ungreased baking sheets. Broil on top rack in oven for 1 to 2 minutes until crisp and browned. Serve warm. Makes about 30 toasts.

1 toast: 51 Calories; 2.6 g Total Fat (1.4 g Mono, 0.6 g Poly, 0.4 g Sat); 0 mg Cholesterol; 6 g Carbohydrate; trace Fibre; 1 g Protein; 94 mg Sodium

Pictured on page 9.

Note: Paste food colouring gives a wider variety of vivid colours. It can be purchased at craft or cake decorating stores.

Ancient Animal Bones

Tender, meaty ribs to eat with your hands. If the children are older, the recipe can easily be doubled.

Meaty pork back ribs (cut into individual ribs)	2 lbs.	900 g
Cold water, to cover		
Ketchup	1/3 cup	75 mL
Cooking molasses	2 tbsp.	30 mL
Dijon mustard (with whole seeds)	1 tbsp.	15 mL
Pepper	1/2 tsp.	2 mL

Put ribs into large pot or Dutch oven. Cover with cold water. Bring to a boil on medium-high. Cover. Reduce heat to medium-low. Simmer for 30 minutes. Drain well.

Combine remaining 4 ingredients in large bowl. Add ribs. Stir to coat well. Arrange in single layer on large baking sheet lined with greased foil. Bake in 350°F (175°C) oven for about 30 minutes, turning once at halftime, until browned. Makes about 18 ribs.

1 rib: 99 Calories; 7.4 g Total Fat (3.3 g Mono, 0.7 g Poly, 2.7 g Sat); 25 mg Cholesterol; 3 g Carbohydrate; trace Fibre; 5 g Protein; 91 mg Sodium

Pictured on page 9.

Prehistoric Fish Scales

Cut yams into paper-thin slices with vegetable peeler. Deep-fry, in batches, in hot (375°F, 190°C) cooking oil for 1 to 2 minutes until crisp and lightly browned. Remove to paper towels to drain. Sprinkle with salt (or seasoned salt).

Pictured on page 9.

Dinosaur Cake

Cute and adorable. Sure to be a hit at any party.

Box of cake mix (2 layer size), your child's favourite flavour	1	1
Sour cream	1 cup	250 mL
Water	1 cup	250 mL
Large eggs	2	2
FLUFFY FROSTING		
Milk	1 1/2 cups	375 mL
All-purpose flour	3 tbsp.	50 mL
Hard margarine (or butter), softened	1 1/2 cups	375 mL
Granulated sugar	1 1/2 cups	375 mL
Vanilla	1 1/2 tsp.	7 mL
Drops of green (or your child's choice) liquid food colouring	10 – 12	10 – 12

Beat first 4 ingredients in large bowl on low until just combined. Beat on high for about 2 minutes until smooth. Line bottoms of 2 lightly greased 8 inch (20 cm) round cake pans with parchment (or waxed) paper. Divide batter evenly between pans. Bake in 350°F (175°C) oven for 25 to 30 minutes until wooden pick inserted in centre comes out clean. Let stand in pans for 10 minutes before inverting onto wire racks. Peel off paper. Turn right side up. Cool completely. Cut according to pattern (see below).

Fluffy Frosting: Gradually whisk milk into flour in small saucepan until smooth. Heat and stir on medium for about 10 minutes until boiling and thickened. Remove from heat. Transfer to small bowl. Cover with plastic wrap directly on surface. Chill until cold.

(continued on next page)

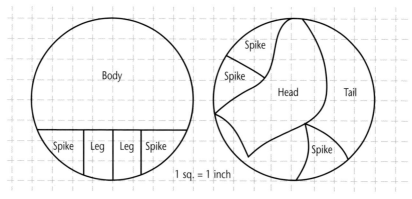

Beat margarine on high until light and fluffy. Gradually add sugar, beating until dissolved. Beat in vanilla. Add milk mixture, 1 tbsp. (15 mL) at a time while beating, until thick and creamy. Makes 4 2/3 cups (1.15 L) frosting. Remove 2/3 cup (150 mL) to small bowl for piping outline and message.

Add food colouring to remaining frosting. Beat until colour is even throughout. Cut cake according to template. Assemble pieces as shown in picture (see below) to form dinosaur. Use small amounts of coloured frosting to secure cake pieces onto cake board (see Tip, page 25) and each other. Spread thin layer of frosting on cake to seal crumbs. Freeze for 25 minutes. Spread with remaining coloured frosting. Fill piping bag with white frosting. Pipe message and accent lines. Serves 12.

1 serving: 569 Calories; 32.9 g Total Fat (19 g Mono, 4.4 g Poly, 7.9 g Sat); 45 mg Cholesterol; 65 g Carbohydrate; trace Fibre; 5 g Protein; 608 mg Sodium

Pictured below.

Variation: Use 2 containers (16 oz., 450 g, each) of commercial frosting for easy decorating and to reduce the fat grams.

Lights! Camera! Action!

This menu is fit for a star! Hold a talent show at your party or rent a karaoke machine. Dine like the rich and famous with these fine selections.

serves 8

Sparkling Raspberry Punch

Colourful Cubes

Ham And Cheese Pinwheels

Chicken Satay Skewers

Shortbread Stars

Chocolate Microphones

Top Left: Sparkling Raspberry Punch, page 16
Centre Left and Bottom Right: Shortbread Stars, page 18
Centre Right: Ham And Cheese Pinwheels, page 16
Bottom Left: Chicken Satay Skewers with Satay Sauce, page 17

Sparkling Raspberry Punch

Rich red punch with sweet raspberry and pineapple flavour.

Pineapple juice	2 cups	500 mL
Package of sweetened raspberry-flavoured drink crystals (about 1 cup, 250 mL)	8 1/2 oz.	240 g
Ginger ale	6 cups	1.5 L

Combine pineapple juice and drink crystals in punch bowl or large pitcher. Stir until drink crystals are dissolved. Chill.

Just before serving, add ginger ale. Makes 8 cups (2 L).

1 cup (250 mL): 217 Calories; 0.1 g Total Fat (0 g Mono, 0 g Poly, 0 g Sat); 0 mg Cholesterol; 55 g Carbohydrate; trace Fibre; 0 g Protein; 50 mg Sodium

Pictured on front cover and on page 15.

Colourful Cubes

Freeze whole raspberries in water in ice cube trays (regular or star-shaped). Just before serving, add to punch.

Ham And Cheese Pinwheels

Rolled up tortillas with a pickle in the centre.

Spreadable cream cheese	2/3 cup	150 mL
Honey mustard	3 tbsp.	50 mL
Large flour tortillas (10 inch, 25 cm, diameter)	2	2
Deli ham slices (about 6 oz., 170 g)	6	6
Small gherkins (straight are best)	8 – 10	8 – 10

Combine cream cheese and mustard in small bowl until smooth.

Spread 1 side of each tortilla with 2 tbsp. (30 mL) cream cheese mixture.

Cover cream cheese mixture with ham slices. Spread ham slices with remaining cream cheese mixture. Line gherkins end to end, about 1 inch (2.5 cm) from bottom of each tortilla. Tightly roll up tortillas from bottom, jelly roll-style, around gherkins. Cut each roll diagonally into 3/4 inch (2 cm) slices. Makes 16 pinwheels.

1 pinwheel: 92 Calories; 5.5 g Total Fat (1.8 g Mono, 0.5 g Poly, 2.8 g Sat); 19 mg Cholesterol; 7 g Carbohydrate; trace Fibre; 4 g Protein; 312 mg Sodium

Pictured on front cover and on page 15.

Chicken Satay Skewers

Serve these delicious skewers with slices of celery and red pepper on the side for a colourful feast.

Boneless, skinless chicken thighs	1 1/2 lbs.	680 g
Bamboo skewers (8 inch, 20 cm, length), soaked in water for 10 minutes	8	8
Salt, sprinkle		
Pepper, sprinkle		
SATAY SAUCE		
Cooking oil	2 tsp.	10 mL
Finely chopped onion	1/3 cup	75 mL
Garlic clove, minced (or 1/4 tsp., 1 mL, powder)	1	1
Ground cumin	1/2 tsp.	2 mL
Prepared chicken broth	3/4 cup	175 mL
Peanut butter (crunchy is best)	1/2 cup	125 mL
Water	3 tbsp.	50 mL
Plum sauce	2 tbsp.	30 mL
Sweet (or regular) chili sauce (optional)	1 tbsp.	15 mL
Soy sauce	2 tsp.	10 mL

Cut chicken crosswise into 1 inch (2.5 cm) wide strips. Thread, accordion-style, onto skewers, leaving about 2 inches (5 cm) on 1 end as handle.

Sprinkle with salt and pepper. Preheat electric grill for 5 minutes or gas barbecue to medium. Cook skewers on greased grill for about 20 minutes, turning occasionally, until chicken is lightly browned and no longer pink inside. Keep warm.

Satay Sauce: Heat cooking oil in medium saucepan on medium. Add onion, garlic and cumin. Cook for about 3 minutes, stirring occasionally, until onion is softened.

Add remaining 6 ingredients. Stir until well combined. Cook for 3 minutes, stirring often, until thickened. Makes 1 2/3 cups (400 mL) sauce. Pour into small dipping bowl. Serve with skewers. Serves 8.

1 serving: 235 Calories; 14.4 g Total Fat (6.2 g Mono, 4 g Poly, 2.9 g Sat); 71 mg Cholesterol; 6 g Carbohydrate; 1 g Fibre; 21 g Protein; 260 mg Sodium

Pictured on front cover and on page 15.

Shortbread Stars

A buttery, melt-in-your-mouth cookie with star power!

Butter (not margarine), softened	1 1/2 cups	375 mL
Icing (confectioner's) sugar	1 cup	250 mL
Egg yolks (large)	2	2
Vanilla	1 tsp.	5 mL
All-purpose flour	3 1/2 cups	875 mL
LEMON GLAZE		
Lemon juice	3 – 4 tbsp.	50 – 60 mL
Icing (confectioner's) sugar	2 cups	500 mL

Food colouring, your choice of 3 colours

Silver dragées (tiny candy balls)

Beat butter and icing sugar in large bowl for about 5 minutes until light and creamy.

Add egg yolks and vanilla. Beat until combined.

Add flour, 1 cup (250 mL) at a time, beating until soft dough forms. Do not overbeat. Roll out dough on lightly floured surface to 1/3 inch (1 cm) thickness. Cut 8 cookies from dough with 5 1/2 inch (14 cm) star-shaped cookie cutter. Repeat with remaining dough, using 2 3/4 inch (7 cm) star-shaped cookie cutter. Place about 1 inch (2.5 cm) apart on lightly greased cookie sheets. Bake in 325°F (160°C) oven for 12 to 15 minutes until firm and edges are lightly golden. Let stand on cookie sheets for 5 minutes before removing to wire racks to cool.

Lemon Glaze: Add enough lemon juice to icing sugar in medium bowl to make smooth, spreadable glaze. Makes about 1 cup (250 mL) glaze. Spoon 2 tbsp. (30 mL) into each of 3 small bowls. Cover remaining glaze with damp cloth when not in use to prevent drying out. Set aside.

Stir enough food colouring into each bowl to make desired shade. Spoon into small piping bags fitted with small plain tips. Ice cookies as desired with 4 colours of glaze.

Decorate cookies with dragées. Let stand on wire racks until set. Do not stack cookies on top of each other. Makes 8 large and 16 small cookies.

1 large cookie: 490 Calories; 25.6 g Total Fat (7.4 g Mono, 1.2 g Poly, 15.5 g Sat); 102 mg Cholesterol; 61 g Carbohydrate; 1 g Fibre; 5 g Protein; 250 mg Sodium

Pictured on front cover and on page 15.

Chocolate Microphones

These sweet treats will make any child feel like a star!

Waffle sugar cones	8	8
Candy-coated chocolate candies (such as Smarties)	1 1/2 cups	375 mL
Chocolate ice cream	2 cups	500 mL
Semi-sweet chocolate baking squares (1 oz., 28 g, each), melted	2	2

Place cones in popsicle mold holder or tall narrow glasses. Divide and put candies into cones.

Fill with ice cream, using 1/4 cup (60 mL) ice cream scoop. Place upright in molds. Freeze.

Spoon melted chocolate into small piping bag fitted with small plain tip. Pipe chocolate over ice cream in grid pattern resembling top of microphone. Return to freezer until chocolate is set. Makes 8 cones.

1 cone: 335 Calories; 15 g Total Fat (2 g Mono, 0.4 g Poly, 3.7 g Sat); 18 mg Cholesterol; 49 g Carbohydrate; 2 g Fibre; 5 g Protein; 99 mg Sodium

Pictured on front cover and below.

Medieval Party

*Take a trip to the Middle Ages. Serve food at
a round table with lots of candlelight and
let the kids eat with their fingers!*

serves 8

Crispy Wedges

Dragon Drumsticks

King Ribs

Buttery Corncobs

Castle Cake

Top Left: Crispy Wedges, page 22
Top Right: Buttery Corncobs, page 24
Bottom: King Ribs, page 23

Crispy Wedges

Potato with a crispy sesame seed coating. Kids can dip them into "dragon blood" ketchup!

Red medium potatoes (with peel), cut into 8 wedges each	4	4
Cooking oil	1 1/2 tbsp.	25 mL
Sesame seeds	1 tbsp.	15 mL
Salt	1/4 tsp.	1 mL
Pepper, sprinkle		

Combine all 5 ingredients in large bowl. Toss until potato wedges are coated. Arrange in single layer on greased baking sheet. Bake in 375°F (190°C) oven for about 60 minutes, turning occasionally, until crisp and golden. Makes 32 wedges.

4 wedges: 85 Calories; 3.2 g Total Fat (1.7 g Mono, 1.1 g Poly, 0.3 g Sat); 0 mg Cholesterol; 13 g Carbohydrate; 1 g Fibre; 2 g Protein; 80 mg Sodium

Pictured on page 21.

Dragon Drumsticks

A crisp coating on tender chicken. Dip into ranch dressing.

Cornflakes cereal	3 cups	750 mL
Envelope of dry onion soup mix	1 1/2 oz.	42 g
Buttermilk (or reconstituted from powder)	1/2 cup	125 mL
Chicken drumsticks (about 2 lbs., 900 g)	8	8

Process cereal and soup mix in blender or food processor until coarse crumbs. Place in shallow dish.

Combine buttermilk and drumsticks in large bowl until drumsticks are coated. Press each drumstick into cereal mixture to coat completely. Arrange in single layer on baking sheet lined with greased foil. Spray surface of drumsticks with cooking spray. Bake in 375°F (190°C) oven for about 40 minutes until no longer pink inside. Makes 8 drumsticks.

1 drumstick: 212 Calories; 11.1 g Total Fat (4.3 g Mono, 2.4 g Poly, 3.1 g Sat); 62 mg Cholesterol; 12 g Carbohydrate; trace Fibre; 15 g Protein; 584 mg Sodium

Pictured on page 23.

King Ribs

Tender, meaty ribs with a pleasant barbecue smokiness and sweet glaze.

Liquid honey	1/2 cup	125 mL
Barbecue sauce	1/2 cup	125 mL
Orange juice	1/4 cup	60 mL
Soy sauce	2 tbsp.	30 mL
Dijon mustard (with whole seeds)	1 tbsp.	15 mL
Pork spareribs (uncut side rack)	2 lbs.	900 g

Combine first 5 ingredients in small bowl.

Place rack of ribs on greased wire rack in foil-lined roasting pan or on foil-lined baking sheet. Brush ribs with glaze. Bake, uncovered, in 375°F (190°C) oven for about 1 1/2 hours, brushing with glaze and turning occasionally, until tender and browned. Cut between each rib bone into individual ribs. Makes about 18 ribs.

1 rib: 160 Calories; 8.2 g Total Fat (3.6 g Mono, 0.8 g Poly, 3 g Sat); 39 mg Cholesterol; 11 g Carbohydrate; trace Fibre; 10 g Protein; 222 mg Sodium

Pictured on page 21.

Dragon Drumsticks, page 22

Buttery Corncobs

Cut 4 ears of fresh corn in half crosswise. Cook in boiling water in large uncovered pot or Dutch oven for about 3 minutes until tender. Drain. Toss in melted butter.

Pictured on page 21.

Castle Cake

Grey medieval icing sets the mood for this tasty treat.

Box of yellow cake mix (2 layer size)	1	1
CASTLE ICING		
Icing (confectioner's) sugar	5 cups	1.25 L
Milk, approximately	1/2 cup	125 mL
Hard margarine (or butter), softened	1/3 cup	75 mL
Blue liquid (or paste) food colouring (see Note)		
Black paste food colouring (see Note)		
Ice cream (sugar) cones (not waffle), 5 inch (12.5 cm) tall	4	4
Package of fruit leather	1/2 oz.	14 g
Stick (and/or waffle) pretzels		
Assorted candies, for decorating (6 – 9 oz., 170 – 255 g), see Candy Note	1 1/2 cups	375 mL

Prepare cake mix according to package directions. Pour batter into greased 9 x 9 inch (22 x 22 cm) pan. It will be very full. Bake in 350°F (175°C) oven for 50 to 55 minutes until wooden pick inserted in centre comes out clean. Let stand in pan for 10 minutes before removing to wire rack to cool completely.

Castle Icing: Beat icing sugar, milk and margarine in large bowl until smooth. Add more icing sugar or milk, if necessary, until spreading consistency. Makes 3 cups (750 mL) icing.

Remove 1/2 cup (125 mL) icing to small bowl. Add enough blue food colouring to make desired colour. Set aside.

Add enough black food colouring to remaining icing to make pale grey colour. Reserve 1/4 cup (60 mL) icing for "gluing" on candies. Cover until ready to use.

(continued on next page)

Carefully cut off top of cake horizontally to remove dome. Invert cake. Cover top and sides of cake with grey icing. Make shield shape on top of cake with blue icing. Ice each ice cream cone with grey icing. Place 1 cone on each corner of cake to make turrets. Secure with grey icing.

Cut fruit leather to make door, turret windows and flags. Use pretzels to make windows and drawbridge. Decorate cake with assorted candies. Cuts into 12 pieces.

1 piece: 516 Calories; 10.7 g Total Fat (5.7 g Mono, 2.5 g Poly, 1.9 g Sat); 1 mg Cholesterol; 105 g Carbohydrate; trace Fibre; 3 g Protein; 372 mg Sodium

Pictured below.

Note: Paste food colouring gives a wider variety of vivid colours. It can be purchased at craft or decorating stores.

Candy Note: Use candies such as black licorice blocks, black licorice string, candy-coated chocolate candies, jawbreakers and silver dragée (ball) candies. Use gummy candies for the dragon in the moat.

Tip: Make cake board using a 12 × 12 inch (30 × 30 cm) piece of cardboard. Cover with a 12 × 12 inch (30 × 30 cm) piece of blue poster board. Secure with tape. Place cake on board. Place pieces of plastic wrap under cake on board to prevent smearing when icing cake. Or purchase blue foam core available at craft or stationery stores.

Spy Party

This clever menu consists of food that is "concealed."
Kids will have fun discovering what each item is.
Keep party guests entertained for hours with
treasure hunts and other "spy" games.

serves 8

Midnight Punch

Cloaked Wieners

Pizza In Disguise

Whodunit Snacks

Ham And Cheese Bombs

Magnifying Glass Cake

Midnight Punch

Combine equal amounts of grape juice and lemon lime soft drink in punch bowl or large pitcher for a dark-as-a-moonlit-night drink.

Pictured on page 27.

Cloaked Wieners

A wiener hidden inside flaky, golden pastry.

Mini European wieners	16	16
Boiling water, to cover		
Package of frozen puff pastry, thawed according to package directions	14 oz.	397 g
Large egg, fork-beaten	1	1
Ketchup, for dipping		
Honey mustard, for dipping		

Cover wieners with boiling water in medium saucepan. Simmer for 5 minutes. Remove from heat. Cover. Let stand for 10 minutes. Drain. Blot dry on paper towel. Cool.

Roll out 1/2 of pastry on lightly floured surface to 12 x 10 inch (30 x 25 cm) rectangle. Cut pastry in half lengthwise. Cut each half crosswise into 4 sections, for a total of 8 pieces.

Place 1 wiener along length in centre of 1 piece of pastry. Lightly brush long sides of pastry with egg. Roll up to enclose wiener. Twist each end tightly together. Repeat with remaining pastry and wieners. Arrange, seam-side down, about 1 inch (2.5 cm) apart on lightly greased baking sheets. Lightly brush tops and sides with egg. Bake in 425°F (220°C) oven for about 15 minutes until golden. Remove to wire rack to cool.

Serve warm with ketchup and honey mustard for dipping. Makes 16 wrapped wieners.

1 wrapped wiener: 251 Calories; 18.5 g Total Fat (6.4 g Mono, 6.3 g Poly, 4.7 g Sat); 32 mg Cholesterol; 13 g Carbohydrate; 0 g Fibre; 7 g Protein; 440 mg Sodium

Pictured on page 27.

Pizza In Disguise

Golden half moons of pastry filled with a mild pizza mixture.

Olive (or cooking) oil	1 tbsp.	15 mL
Finely chopped onion	1/2 cup	125 mL
Garlic clove, minced (or 1/4 tsp., 1 mL, powder)	1	1
Finely chopped green pepper	1/2 cup	125 mL
Pizza sauce	1/2 cup	125 mL
Chopped deli salami (or ham) slices (about 4 oz., 113 g)	3/4 cup	175 mL
Grated part-skim mozzarella cheese	1 cup	250 mL
Frozen dough dinner rolls, thawed but not risen (see Note)	8	8
Large egg, fork-beaten	1	1

Heat olive oil in large frying pan on medium. Add onion, garlic and green pepper. Cook, stirring often, until onion is softened. Turn into large bowl. Cool.

Add next 3 ingredients. Mix well.

Roll out each dinner roll on lightly floured surface to about 6 inch (15 cm) circle. Spread 1/4 cup (60 mL) filling on 1/2 of each circle, leaving 1/2 inch (12 mm) edge. Fold other halves of dough over filling. Press edges together with fork to seal well. Place on greased baking sheet.

Brush tops and sides with egg. Bake in 375°F (190°C) oven for about 20 minutes until golden brown. Let stand on baking sheet for 5 minutes before removing to serving plate. Serve warm. Makes 8 calzones.

1 calzone: 215 Calories; 11.4 g Total Fat (5.3 g Mono, 1.2 g Poly, 4.2 g Sat); 49 mg Cholesterol; 20 g Carbohydrate; 1 g Fibre; 9 g Protein; 446 mg Sodium

Pictured on page 27.

Note: There will be dough for 12 buns in a 16 oz. (454 g) package of frozen dinner roll dough. Thaw all rolls at same time, using 8 for this recipe and bake remaining 4 rolls for dinner.

Whodunit Snacks

Cut question-mark shapes out of Cheddar cheese and bread slices.

Pictured on page 27.

Ham And Cheese Bombs

A great combination of smooth texture and salty flavour.

Block of cream cheese, softened	8 oz.	250 g
Finely chopped lean ham (about 3 oz., 85 g)	2/3 cup	150 mL
Grated medium Cheddar cheese	1/2 cup	125 mL
Soy sauce	1 tsp.	5 mL
Sesame seeds, toasted until deep golden (see Note)	1/2 cup	125 mL
Finely chopped fresh parsley	1 tbsp.	15 mL
Parsley stems (with leaves)	24	24

Mix first 4 ingredients in medium bowl. Roll into balls, using 1 tbsp. (15 mL) for each.

Combine sesame seeds and chopped parsley in small shallow dish. Roll each ball until well coated. Place on ungreased baking sheet. Chill for at least 2 hours until firm and up to 2 days in airtight container.

Put 1 parsley stem into each ball to resemble fuse just before serving. Makes about 24 bombs.

1 bomb: 72 Calories; 6.3 g Total Fat (2 g Mono, 0.9 g Poly, 3.1 g Sat); 17 mg Cholesterol; 1 g Carbohydrate; trace Fibre; 3 g Protein; 158 mg Sodium

Pictured on page 27.

Note: To toast sesame seeds, place in single layer in ungreased shallow pan. Bake in 350°F (175°C) oven for 5 to 10 minutes, stirring or shaking often, until desired doneness.

Magnifying Glass Cake

A large magnifying glass for all your young spies to snack on.

Box of cake mix (2 layer size), your child's favourite flavour	1	1
Black paste food colouring (see Note)		
Container of vanilla (or white) frosting	16 oz.	450 g
Black licorice string (or dark-coloured fruit leather)	10	10
Chocolate-covered Swiss rolls (optional)	3	3
Assorted candies, for decorating		
Tube of dark-coloured decorating gel	2/3 oz.	19 g

(continued on next page)

Prepare cake mix according to package directions. Line bottom of lightly greased 12 inch (30 cm) deep-dish pizza pan with parchment (or waxed) paper. Pour batter into pan. Spread in even layer. Bake in 350°F (175°C) oven for about 30 minutes until wooden pick inserted in centre comes out clean. Let stand in pan for 10 minutes. Remove cake and discard paper. Carefully cut off top of cake to remove dome. Cool completely. Invert cake onto 1 end of 20 × 13 inch (50 × 33 cm) tray or covered cake board, leaving room for handle.

Stir very small amount of food colouring into frosting until very light grey. Ice top and side of cake.

Line circumference of cake with black licorice string to completely cover side.

Line up Swiss rolls end-to-end against cake to form handle. Arrange candies on top of cake in shape of eye. Spell mirror-image message on cake using decorating gel. Cuts into 16 wedges.

1 wedge: 295 Calories; 9.7 g Total Fat (4 g Mono, 2 g Poly, 1.9 g Sat); 1 mg Cholesterol; 51 g Carbohydrate; 0 g Fibre; 2 g Protein; 259 mg Sodium

Pictured below.

Note: Paste food colouring gives a wider variety of vivid colours. It can be purchased at craft or decorating stores.

Haunted Halloween

A frightening menu not for the faint of heart! Slimy brains, a witch's brew and other fun items will get our little ghouls and goblins in the Halloween spirit.

serves 6

Witches' Cauldrons

Mummy Skins

Swamp Cups

Custard Brains

Halloween Apples!

Top Left: Halloween Apples!, page 36
Top Right: Witches' Cauldrons, page 34
Centre: Mummy Skins with Barf Sauce, page 34
Bottom: Swamp Cups, page 35

Witches' Cauldrons

Spooky looking—but delicious to drink!

Cola beverage	6 cups	1.5 L
Scoops of vanilla ice cream	6	6
Tube of red glossy decorating gel	2/3 oz.	19 g
Long gummy snakes	18	18

Pour cola into six 8 oz. (227 mL) glasses. Add 1 scoop of ice cream to each glass. Carefully stir until froth forms on top.

Drizzle with decorating gel. Drape 3 gummy snakes over rim of each glass. Serves 6.

1 serving: 280 Calories; 7.8 g Total Fat (2.2 g Mono, 0.3 g Poly, 4.7 g Sat); 31 mg Cholesterol; 52 g Carbohydrate; 0 g Fibre; 3 g Protein; 91 mg Sodium

Pictured on page 33.

Mummy Skins

Crispy potato skins. Delicious when dunked in warm Barf Sauce!

Whole medium potatoes (with peel)	3	3
Water		
Salt	1/4 tsp.	1 mL
Cooking spray		
Salt, sprinkle		
BARF SAUCE		
Grated medium Cheddar cheese	1/2 cup	125 mL
Mild salsa	1/2 cup	125 mL
Sour cream	3 tbsp.	50 mL

Cook potatoes in water and salt in large saucepan until just tender. Drain. Let stand until cool enough to handle. Cut down around length of each potato 4 to 5 times, removing about 1/4 inch (6 mm) slice of "flesh" and skin with each cut. Slice remaining core of each potato thinly lengthwise.

Place potato slices and skins, skin-side down, on greased baking sheet. Spray liberally with cooking spray. Sprinkle with salt. Bake in 425°F (220°C) oven for about 30 minutes, turning once, until crisp and golden.

(continued on next page)

Barf Sauce: Combine cheese and salsa in small saucepan. Heat and stir on medium-low for 3 to 5 minutes until cheese is almost melted. Remove from heat.

Add sour cream to cheese mixture. Whisk until combined. Makes 3/4 cup (175 mL) sauce. Serve warm with skins. Serves 6.

1 serving: 111 Calories; 4.5 g Total Fat (1.2 g Mono, 0.2 g Poly, 2.8 g Sat); 13 mg Cholesterol; 14 g Carbohydrate; 2 g Fibre; 5 g Protein; 129 mg Sodium

Pictured on page 33.

Swamp Cups

Mild enough that kids will actually enjoy eating broccoli!

Slices of white sandwich bread, crusts removed	12	12
Hard margarine (or butter), melted	2 tbsp.	30 mL
Hard margarine (or butter)	2 tbsp.	30 mL
Finely chopped onion	1/3 cup	75 mL
All-purpose flour	2 tbsp.	30 mL
Homogenized milk	1 1/4 cups	300 mL
Finely chopped broccoli florets	3/4 cup	175 mL
Grated medium Cheddar cheese	1/2 cup	125 mL
Large eggs, fork-beaten	2	2
Bacon slices, cooked crisp and crumbled	4	4
Ground nutmeg (optional)	1/8 tsp.	0.5 mL

Roll out each bread slice to flatten. Brush both sides of each slice with first amount of margarine. Press into muffin pan so each slice comes over top of muffin cup to form irregularly shaped edge. Bake in 350°F (175°C) for 10 to 15 minutes until lightly golden. Let stand in pan until cool.

Melt second amount of margarine in medium saucepan on medium. Add onion. Cook for 3 to 5 minutes, stirring often, until softened.

Add flour. Heat and stir until well combined. Gradually stir in milk. Add broccoli. Cook and stir until boiling and thickened. Remove from heat.

Add remaining 4 ingredients. Stir until cheese is melted. Spoon 2 1/2 tbsp. (37 mL) into each bread cup. Bake in 350°F (175°C) oven for about 15 minutes until set. Serve warm or cold. Makes 12 swamp cups.

1 swamp cup: 110 Calories; 8.4 g Total Fat (4.1 g Mono, 0.7 g Poly, 3.1 g Sat); 47 mg Cholesterol; 4 g Carbohydrate; trace Fibre; 4 g Protein; 147 mg Sodium

Pictured on page 33.

Custard Brains

Wormy custard looks totally gross as "brains" suspended in red jelly. Kids will think it's gross (but fun)!

Custard powder	1/4 cup	60 mL
Milk	1/4 cup	60 mL
Granulated sugar	2 tbsp.	30 mL
Milk	1 1/3 cups	325 mL
Boiling water	2 cups	500 mL
Packages of raspberry (or strawberry) flavoured jelly powder (gelatin), 3 oz., 85 g, each	2	2

Stir first 3 ingredients in medium saucepan until smooth.

Gradually stir in second amount of milk. Heat and stir on medium for about 5 minutes until boiling and slightly thickened. Remove from heat. Let stand for 5 minutes. Stir. Cover with plastic wrap directly on surface to prevent skin from forming.

Combine boiling water and jelly powder in heatproof pitcher. Stir until jelly powder is dissolved. Let stand at room temperature for 1 1/2 to 2 hours until almost set. Divide evenly among six 8 oz. (227 mL) clear wide glasses. Stir custard. Spoon into small freezer bag. Snip small hole from corner of bag. Pipe custard into jelly mixture, back and forth, around and around, to make "brain-like" patterns. Cover each glass with plastic wrap. Chill for at least 3 hours until set. Serves 6.

1 serving: 183 Calories; 0.7 g Total Fat (0.2 g Mono, 0 g Poly, 0.4 g Sat); 3 mg Cholesterol; 41 g Carbohydrate; 0 g Fibre; 4 g Protein; 168 mg Sodium

Pictured on page 37.

Halloween Apples!

Use commercial candy apples or caramel wraps for a classic trick or treat snack.

Pictured on page 33.

Mexican Madness

Don the sombreros and break out the piñatas for this party! These vibrant recipes are flavourful but not too spicy. Almost as much fun to prepare as to eat.

serves 8

Limbo Limeonade

Guacamole

Mind-Your-Own Burritos

Mile High Nachos

Fiesta Ice Cream

Crazy Corn Salsa

Top Right: Fiesta Ice Cream, page 42
Centre Left and Bottom Centre: Crazy Corn Salsa, page 43
Centre: Guacamole, page 40
Bottom Right: Mind-Your-Own Burritos, page 41

Limbo Limeonade

Refreshing, but not too sweet. Make a day ahead.

Water	8 cups	2 L
Granulated sugar	1 1/2 cups	375 mL
Lime juice (fresh is best)	1/2 cup	125 mL
Lemon juice (fresh is best)	1/2 cup	125 mL
Granulated sugar	1/3 cup	75 mL
Drop of green (or yellow) food colouring	1	1
Lime wedge (or water)		
Thin lime slices, halved, for garnish	4	4

Heat and stir water and first amount of sugar in large saucepan on medium for about 5 minutes until sugar is dissolved. Remove from heat.

Add lime and lemon juices. Pour into large pitcher. Cover. Chill overnight.

Shake second amount of sugar and food colouring in small jar with tight-fitting lid until evenly coloured. Spread evenly in saucer.

Dampen rims of eight 8 oz. (227 mL) glasses with lime wedge. Dip rim of each glass into sugar mixture.

Place 1 lime slice half on edge of each glass. Stir limeonade. Carefully pour into each glass, avoiding rim. Serves 8.

1 serving: 196 Calories; 0 g Total Fat (0 g Mono, 0 g Poly, 0 g Sat); 0 mg Cholesterol; 51 g Carbohydrate; trace Fibre; 0 g Protein; 1 mg Sodium

Pictured on page 43.

Guacamole

Purchase commercial guacamole in the deli department of your local grocery store. If you choose to make your own guacamole, be sure to buy ripe avocados.

Pictured on page 39.

Mind-Your-Own Burritos

Kids will have fun assembling these tasty Mexican treats. Have lots of napkins!

Lemon (or lime) juice	2 tbsp.	30 mL
Olive (or cooking) oil	1 tbsp.	15 mL
Garlic clove, minced (or 1/4 tsp., 1 mL, powder)	1	1
Salt	1/4 tsp.	1 mL
Boneless, skinless chicken breast halves, cut into thin strips	1 lb.	454 g
Salsa	1 cup	250 mL
Can of refried beans (optional), warmed	14 oz.	398 mL
Grated mild Cheddar cheese	1 cup	250 mL
Chopped tomato	1 cup	250 mL
Finely sliced green or red pepper (or shredded iceberg lettuce, packed)	1 cup	250 mL
Crazy Corn Salsa, page 43 (optional)		
Sour cream (optional)		
Large flour tortillas (10 inch, 25 cm, diameter), warmed (see Note)	8	8

Combine first 4 ingredients in large bowl.

Add chicken. Turn to coat. Cover. Chill for 30 to 60 minutes.

Drain and discard marinade. Place chicken on large plate. Brush liberally with salsa. Preheat electric grill for 5 minutes or gas barbecue to medium. Cook chicken on greased grill for about 10 minutes, turning occasionally and brushing with salsa, until chicken is no longer pink inside. Cut chicken into thin strips. Keep warm.

Put chicken and next 6 ingredients into 7 separate small bowls.

To assemble, place fillings down centre of tortilla. Roll up to enclose fillings. Makes 8 burritos.

1 burrito: 293 Calories; 10.8 g Total Fat (4.1 g Mono, 1.8 g Poly, 4.1 g Sat); 49 mg Cholesterol; 28 g Carbohydrate; 2 g Fibre; 21 g Protein; 458 mg Sodium

Pictured on page 39.

Note: To warm and soften tortillas, wrap in foil or damp tea towel. Heat in 200°F (95°C) oven for about 10 minutes.

Mile High Nachos

Piled high with loads of toppings!

Cooking oil	2 tsp.	10 mL
Extra lean ground beef	3/4 lb.	340 g
Water	3/4 cup	175 mL
Salsa	1/2 cup	125 mL
Tomato paste	2 tbsp.	30 mL
Envelope of taco seasoning mix	1 1/4 oz.	35 g
Bag of tortilla chips	12 oz.	340 g
Grated medium Cheddar cheese	2 cups	500 mL
Shredded iceberg lettuce, packed	1 cup	250 mL
Diced, seeded tomato	1 cup	250 mL
Salsa	1/2 cup	125 mL
Sour cream	1/2 cup	125 mL

Heat cooking oil in large frying pan on medium-high. Add ground beef. Scramble-fry for about 5 minutes until no pink remains. Drain.

Add next 4 ingredients. Stir. Reduce heat to medium. Cook for about 6 minutes, stirring occasionally, until thickened and no liquid remains.

Arrange 1/2 of tortilla chips on 12 inch (30 cm) foil-lined pizza pan. Spoon 1/2 of beef mixture over chips.

Sprinkle with 1/2 of cheese. Repeat with remaining chips, beef mixture and cheese. This will be high. Broil on centre rack for 2 to 5 minutes until cheese is melted.

Sprinkle with lettuce and tomato.

Serve with salsa and sour cream. Serves 8.

1 serving: 462 Calories; 28.6 g Total Fat (12.4 g Mono, 2.5 g Poly, 11.3 g Sat); 59 mg Cholesterol; 34 g Carbohydrate; 4 g Fibre; 20 g Protein; 783 mg Sodium

Pictured on page 43.

Fiesta Ice Cream

Serve small wedges of watermelon and cantaloupe with large scoop of vanilla ice cream.

Pictured on page 39.

Crazy Corn Salsa

A quick and easy salsa for all to enjoy. Serve at room temperature for best flavour.

Medium tomatoes, seeded and diced	2	2
Can of kernel corn, drained	19 oz.	540 mL
Chopped fresh parsley	2 tbsp.	30 mL
Olive (or cooking) oil	1 tbsp.	15 mL
Lime (or lemon) juice	1 tbsp.	15 mL
Garlic clove, minced (or 1/4 tsp., 1 mL, powder)	1	1
Salt	1/4 tsp.	1 mL

Combine all 7 ingredients in medium bowl. Makes 3 cups (750 mL) salsa.

2 tbsp. (30 mL): 21 Calories; 0.7 g Total Fat (0.4 g Mono, 0.1 g Poly, 0.1 g Sat); 0 mg Cholesterol; 4 g Carbohydrate; trace Fibre; 1 g Protein; 72 mg Sodium

Pictured on page 39.

Top: Limbo Limeonade, page 40   Bottom: Mile High Nachos, page 42

Proud To Be...

*Get your kids in the mood for a fun-filled celebration!
Whatever the reason, whoop it up with style and spirit! Invite
everyone to come wearing country, school or team colours.*

serves 8

Cranberry Cooler

Mini Burgers

Bacon Potato Salad

Cheese Snacks

Jelly Bean Cake

Top: Jelly Bean Cake, page 49
Centre Right: Mini Burgers, page 46
Bottom Left: Bacon Potato Salad, page 48

Cranberry Cooler

Perfect refreshment for a sunny, hot celebration.

Cranberry juice	4 cups	1 L
Ginger ale	4 cups	1 L
Pineapple juice	2 cups	500 mL

Combine all 3 ingredients in large pitcher. Makes 10 cups (2.5 L).

1 cup (250 mL): 127 Calories; 0.1 g Total Fat (0 g Mono, 0 g Poly, 0 g Sat); 0 mg Cholesterol; 32 g Carbohydrate; trace Fibre; 0 g Protein; 12 mg Sodium

Pictured on page 47.

Mini Burgers

Kid-sized burgers with a nice barbecue taste.

Lean ground beef	1 lb.	454 g
Grated mild Cheddar cheese	1/2 cup	125 mL
Finely chopped onion	1/3 cup	75 mL
Tomato paste (or ketchup)	2 tbsp.	30 mL
Salt	1/4 tsp.	1 mL
Hard margarine (or butter), softened	3 tbsp.	50 mL
Garlic powder	1 tsp.	5 mL
Tray buns (or small dinner rolls), cut in half	8	8
Barbecue sauce	1/3 cup	75 mL
Medium tomatoes, sliced	2	2
Shredded iceberg lettuce, packed	1 cup	250 mL

Combine first 5 ingredients in medium bowl. Divide and shape into 8 patties. Preheat electric grill for 5 minutes or gas barbecue to medium. Cook patties on greased grill for 3 to 4 minutes per side until no longer pink inside.

Combine margarine and garlic powder in small bowl. Spread onto cut sides of each bun. Grill cut sides of buns for 1 to 2 minutes until golden.

(continued on next page)

Spread bottom half of each bun with about 1 1/2 tsp. (7 mL) barbecue sauce. Layer with 1 hamburger patty, tomato slice and lettuce. Top each with remaining half of bun. Makes 8 burgers.

1 burger: 299 Calories; 17.8 g Total Fat (8.4 g Mono, 1.3 g Poly, 6.4 g Sat); 40 mg Cholesterol; 19 g Carbohydrate; 2 g Fibre; 16 g Protein; 452 mg Sodium

Pictured on page 45.

Centre: Cranberry Coolers, page 46   Bottom Right: Cheese Snacks, page 48

Bacon Potato Salad

Creamy potato salad with mild flavours just for kids.

Red baby potatoes (with peel), halved	1 1/2 lbs.	680 g
Water		
Salt	1/4 tsp.	1 mL
Sour cream	1/2 cup	125 mL
Canadian back bacon slices (about 3 oz., 85 g), cooked almost crisp and chopped	6	6
Chopped fresh chives (or 2 1/4 tsp., 11 mL, dried)	3 tbsp.	50 mL
Honey mustard	2 tbsp.	30 mL

Cook potatoes in water and salt until just tender. Drain well. Cool. Transfer to large bowl.

Combine remaining 4 ingredients in small bowl. Add to potatoes. Stir until coated. Chill for 3 hours. Makes 4 cups (1 L).

1/2 cup (125 mL): 109 Calories; 2.9 g Total Fat (0.9 g Mono, 0.3 g Poly, 1.5 g Sat); 13 mg Cholesterol; 17 g Carbohydrate; 1 g Fibre; 4 g Protein; 134 mg Sodium

Pictured on page 45.

Cheese Snacks

Cut mozzarella cheese into 1/2 to 3/4 inch (1.2 to 2 cm) cubes. Cut cherry tomatoes in half. Place wooden pick through 1 tomato half and 1 cheese cube. Use small wooden pick with your country's flag or favourite sports team colours on top!

Pictured on page 47.

Jelly Bean Cake

Celebrate with this bright, festive cake! Use jelly beans to create any design from a country's flag to a team logo to a family coat of arms. Serve with ice cream.

Box of white cake mix (2 layer size)	1	1
Container of vanilla frosting	16 oz.	450 g
Small red (or your choice) jelly beans	1 1/2 cups	375 mL
Small white (or your choice) jelly beans	1 1/4 cups	300 mL

Prepare cake batter according to package directions. Pour into greased 9 x 13 inch (22 x 33 cm) pan. Bake in 350°F (175°C) oven for about 30 minutes until wooden pick inserted in centre comes out clean. Let stand in pan for 10 minutes before removing to wire rack to cool.

Carefully cut off top of cake horizontally to remove dome. Secure to cake board or large platter with small amount of frosting. Cover top and sides with frosting.

Trace maple leaf (or other design) on top of cake with tip of wooden pick. Fill in design with enough red jelly beans to cover. Fill in background of cake with white jelly beans. Line remaining red jelly beans around bottom edges of cake in icing. Cuts into 16 pieces.

1 piece: 342 Calories; 5.2 g Total Fat (2.4 g Mono, 1.5 g Poly, 0.9 g Sat); 0 mg Cholesterol; 74 g Carbohydrate; 0 g Fibre; 2 g Protein; 242 mg Sodium

Pictured on page 45.

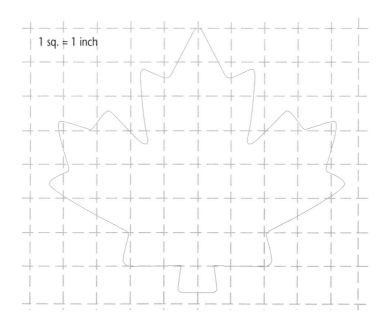

1 sq. = 1 inch

Pseudo Sushi

Introduce party guests to something new and inviting with these Asian-inspired recipes. Encourage kids to eat with chopsticks; teach them origami; and have fun with the decor.

serves 6

Make-Your-Own Rice Bowls

Crispy Rice Sushi

Spring Rolls

Top: Spring Rolls, page 53
Top Right, Centre Left and Bottom Left: Make-Your-Own Rice Bowls, page 52
Centre Left: Crispy Rice Sushi, page 53

Make-Your-Own Rice Bowls

Yummy chicken, crisp vegetables and white rice. Don't forget the chopsticks!

Boneless, skinless chicken breast halves, thinly sliced	3/4 lb.	340 g
Teriyaki stir-fry sauce	3 tbsp.	50 mL
Finely grated, peeled gingerroot (optional)	1/4 tsp.	1 mL
Garlic clove, minced (or 1/4 tsp., 1 mL, powder)	1	1
Water	3 cups	750 mL
Salt	1 tsp.	5 mL
Long grain white rice	1 1/2 cups	375 mL
Cooking oil	2 tsp.	10 mL
Bean sprouts, trimmed and coarsely chopped	1 cup	250 mL
Large carrot, cut julienne	1	1
Julienned snow peas	3/4 cup	175 mL
Thinly sliced green or red pepper	3/4 cup	175 mL
Thinly sliced green onion	1/4 cup	60 mL
Plum sauce, teriyaki sauce, soy sauce or Indonesian sweet (or thick) soy sauce (optional), for drizzling		

Combine first 4 ingredients in medium bowl. Cover. Chill for at least 30 minutes.

Combine water and salt in large saucepan. Bring to a boil. Add rice. Stir. Cover. Reduce heat to low. Cook for 15 minutes. Remove from heat. Do not lift lid. Let stand for 5 minutes. Fluff with fork.

Heat wok or large frying pan on medium-high until hot. Add cooking oil. Add chicken and marinade. Stir-fry for about 5 minutes until no longer pink inside. Keep warm.

Divide rice among 6 individual serving bowls. Divide chicken over rice. Place next 6 ingredients on sectioned serving platter or in separate small bowls. Let children add toppings as desired to their own rice bowls. Serves 6.

1 serving: 290 Calories; 3 g Total Fat (1.3 g Mono, 0.8 g Poly, 0.5 g Sat); 33 mg Cholesterol; 46 g Carbohydrate; 2 g Fibre; 18 g Protein; 757 mg Sodium

Pictured on page 51.

Crispy Rice Sushi

Colourful, sweet sushi rolls. Can be easily made ahead and sliced before serving.

Hard margarine (or butter)	3 tbsp.	50 mL
Miniature white marshmallows	3 cups	750 mL
Crisp rice cereal	4 cups	1 L
Hard margarine (or butter), softened	1 tbsp.	15 mL
Individual fruit strips (such as Fruit Roll-Ups), your child's favourite flavours (1/2 oz., 14 g, each)	8	8
Gummy worms (or licorice), your child's favourite flavours		
Chocolate sprinkles (optional)	1/4 cup	60 mL
Green (or purple) sprinkles (optional)	1/4 cup	60 mL

Trace 6 x 12 inch (15 x 30 cm) rectangle on piece of parchment (or waxed) paper. Turn over. Set aside. Melt first amount of margarine in Dutch oven on medium. Add marshmallows. Heat and stir for about 3 minutes until marshmallows are smooth and melted. Remove from heat.

Add cereal. Mix well. Divide into 2 portions. Keep 1 portion warm in oven preheated to 200°F (95°C) and then turned off.

Grease hands well with about 1 tsp. (5 mL) second amount of margarine. Spread first portion of marshmallow mixture with hands to fit rectangle. Grease hands with remaining margarine as needed to prevent sticking. Pack down in even layer.

Lay fruit strips, side-by-side, in even layer on marshmallow mixture. Trim if needed. Place gummy worms on fruit strips in 2 or 3 horizontal rows. Starting at edge nearest to you, roll up snuggly, using paper as a guide. Gently heat roll to soften in warm oven.

Coat with sprinkles. Set aside. Repeat with remaining ingredients. Let stand for 30 minutes until firm. Each roll cuts into 12 slices, for a total of 24 "sushi."

1 sushi: 72 Calories; 2 g Total Fat (1.3 g Mono, 0.2 g Poly, 0.4 g Sat); 0 mg Cholesterol; 13 g Carbohydrate; trace Fibre; 1 g Protein; 80 mg Sodium

Pictured on page 51.

Spring Rolls

Prepare commercial spring rolls according to package directions. Serve with desired dipping sauce.

Pictured on page 51.

Kids Only Camp Out

This is a wonderful menu to prepare for a group of backyard campers. Feed them a hearty meal and send them to their tents with a few munchies.

serves 4

Potato Salsa Salad

Lemonade

Snack-To-Go

Cheesy Sausages

Marshmallow Fruit Kabobs

Chocolate Rocks

Top Left: Potato Salsa Salad, page 56
Centre Right: Snack-To-Go, page 57
Bottom Left: Cheesy Sausages, page 57

Potato Salsa Salad

A tangy, colourful potato salad that's a bit different from the traditional kind.

Baby potatoes (with peel), halved	1 lb.	454 g
Salt	1/2 tsp.	2 mL
Water		
Olive (or cooking) oil	2 tbsp.	30 mL
Chopped fresh parsley (or 1 1/2 tsp., 7 mL, flakes)	2 tbsp.	30 mL
Lemon (or lime) juice	2 tbsp.	30 mL
Granulated sugar	1/2 tsp.	2 mL
Chili powder	1/2 tsp.	2 mL
Garlic clove, minced (or 1/4 tsp., 1 mL, powder)	1	1
Salt	1/4 tsp.	1 mL
Medium tomatoes, quartered and chopped	2	2
Chopped green onion	3 tbsp.	50 mL

Cook potatoes in salt and water until just tender. Drain well. Place in large bowl.

Combine next 7 ingredients in small bowl. Add to potatoes. Toss to coat.

Add tomato and green onion. Toss gently. Serve warm or cold. Makes 4 cups (1 L).

1/2 cup (125 mL) serving: 83 Calories; 3.6 g Total Fat (2.5 g Mono, 0.4 g Poly, 0.5 g Sat); 0 mg Cholesterol; 12 g Carbohydrate; 1 g Fibre; 2 g Protein; 84 mg Sodium

Pictured on page 55.

Lemonade

Put lemonade into camp cup or water bottle with child's name on it.

Pictured on page 59.

Snack-To-Go

Put trail mix or popped popcorn into small plastic containers.

Pictured on page 55.

Cheesy Sausages

Top cooked sausages with grated mild Cheddar cheese.

Pictured on page 55.

Marshmallow Fruit Kabobs

Sweet, grilled fruit with soft, gooey marshmallows. Use long skewers to provide a "handle" to hold when eating.

Medium banana, cut into 8 pieces	1	1
Pieces of fresh pineapple (or canned pineapple chunks, drained)	8	8
Large white (or coloured) marshmallows	8	8
Bamboo skewers (12 inch, 30 cm, length), soaked in water for 10 minutes	4	4
Hard margarine (or butter), melted	1 tbsp.	15 mL

Divide and thread banana, pineapple and marshmallow alternately onto skewers, pushing close together, leaving about 2 inches (5 cm) on 1 end as handle.

Brush all sides with margarine. Preheat barbecue to medium. Cook skewers on greased grill for about 1 minute on each side until marshmallows are starting to soften and brown. Makes 4 kabobs.

1 kabob: 113 Calories; 3.2 g Total Fat (1.9 g Mono, 0.4 g Poly, 0.7 g Sat); 0 mg Cholesterol; 22 g Carbohydrate; trace Fibre; 1 g Protein; 41 mg Sodium

Pictured on page 59.

Chocolate Rocks

Chocolatey good, with candy sprinkles and crunchy cereal. Doubles easily.

Milk chocolate bars (3 1/2 oz., 100 g, each), chopped	3	3
Hard margarine (or butter)	1/2 cup	125 mL
Crispy rice cereal	1 cup	250 mL
Icing (confectioner's) sugar	1/3 cup	75 mL
Medium unsweetened coconut, toasted (see Note)	1/4 cup	60 mL
Miniature multi-coloured marshmallows	1/4 cup	60 mL
Star-shaped (or other) candy sprinkles (optional)	1 tbsp.	15 mL

Heat chocolate and margarine in heavy medium saucepan on lowest heat, stirring often, until almost melted. Do not overheat. Remove from heat. Stir until smooth.

Add next 4 ingredients. Mix well. Place cupcake liners in muffin cups. Divide and spoon about 1/4 cup (60 mL) chocolate mixture into each liner, piling up mixture to resemble a rock. Do not flatten.

Decorate with sprinkles while still warm. Chill for at least 3 hours or overnight. Makes 8 rocks.

1 rock: 360 Calories; 25.5 g Total Fat (7.3 g Mono, 0.9 g Poly, 16.1 g Sat); 41 mg Cholesterol; 32 g Carbohydrate; 1 g Fibre; 3 g Protein; 194 mg Sodium

Pictured on page 59.

Note: To toast coconut, place in ungreased shallow pan. Bake in 350°F (175°C) oven for 5 to 10 minutes, stirring or shaking often, until desired doneness.

Top Left: Marshmallow Fruit Kabobs, page 57
Top Right: Lemonade, page 56
Bottom: Chocolate Rocks, above

Picnic In The Park

Pack a Frisbee, a beach volleyball and these tasty make-ahead items to enjoy a beautiful day in the park. This menu can transport easily, so the party goes where you go. Be sure to keep everything well chilled until you're ready to eat.

serves 6

Lemon Berry Delight

Crunchy Chicken Wraps

Rainbow Treat Cookies

Picnic Finger Food

Top Left: Picnic Finger Food, page 63
Top Right: Lemon Berry Delight, page 62
Centre: Rainbow Treat Cookies, page 63
Bottom: Crunchy Chicken Wraps, page 62

Lemon Berry Delight

A refreshing drink that is simply delightful!

Lemonade	8 cups	2 L
Sliced fresh strawberries (about 15)	1 1/2 cups	375 mL
Ice cubes	12 – 14	12 – 14

Process lemonade, strawberries and ice cubes in blender, in 2 batches, until small chunks. Pour into large insulated drink container. Makes 10 cups (2.5 L).

1 cup (250 mL): 92 Calories; 0.1 g Total Fat (0 g Mono, 0.1 g Poly, 0 g Sat); 0 mg Cholesterol; 24 g Carbohydrate; trace Fibre; 0 g Protein; 7 mg Sodium

Pictured on page 61.

Crunchy Chicken Wraps

These wraps are filled with flavour, yet are not messy to eat.

Block of cream cheese, softened	4 oz.	113 g
Salad dressing (or mayonnaise)	2 tbsp.	30 mL
Lemon juice	1 tbsp.	15 mL
Chopped roasted (or barbecued) chicken, skin removed	2 cups	500 mL
Coarsely chopped raisins	2/3 cup	150 mL
Finely chopped celery	2/3 cup	150 mL
Finely chopped red pepper	1/2 cup	125 mL
Slivered almonds, toasted (see Note)	1/3 cup	75 mL
Salt, just a pinch		
Large flour tortillas (10 inch, 25 cm, diameter)	3	3

Beat first 3 ingredients in large bowl until smooth.

Add next 6 ingredients. Stir until well combined.

Spoon 1 cup (250 mL) chicken mixture into centre of each tortilla, leaving 1 1/2 inch (3.8 cm) edge. Fold sides over filling. Roll up from bottom to enclose filling. Slice in half diagonally. Serves 6.

1 serving: 362 Calories; 18.9 g Total Fat (7.9 g Mono, 3.4 g Poly, 6.3 g Sat); 68 mg Cholesterol; 29 g Carbohydrate; 2 g Fibre; 20 g Protein; 250 mg Sodium

Pictured on page 61.

Note: To toast almonds, place in single layer in ungreased shallow pan. Bake in 350°F (175°C) oven for 5 to 10 minutes, stirring or shaking often, until desired doneness.

Rainbow Treat Cookies

A hard vanilla cookie baked crispy golden, filled with colourful bits.

Package of yellow cake mix (1 layer size)	1	1
Cornflakes cereal, lightly crushed	2/3 cup	150 mL
Mini rainbow-coloured baking chips (see Note)	1/2 cup	125 mL
Quick-cooking rolled oats (not instant)	1/3 cup	75 mL
Brown sugar, packed	1/4 cup	60 mL
Hard margarine (or butter), melted	1/4 cup	60 mL
Large egg, fork-beaten	1	1

Combine first 5 ingredients in medium bowl.

Add margarine and egg. Mix until soft dough forms. Shape into balls, using 1 tbsp. (15 mL) for each. Arrange 3 inches (7.5 cm) apart on greased cookie sheet. Bake in 350°F (175°C) oven for 10 to 12 minutes until golden. Let stand on cookie sheet for 5 minutes before removing to wire rack to cool. Makes 16 cookies.

1 cookie: 211 Calories; 7.3 g Total Fat (3.7 g Mono, 1.8 g Poly, 1.3 g Sat); 14 mg Cholesterol; 34 g Carbohydrate; trace Fibre; 2 g Protein; 297 mg Sodium

Pictured on page 61.

Note: If these are difficult to find, purchase colourful, candy-coated chocolate baking bits (such as miniature M & Ms).

Picnic Finger Food

Take along green and red grapes, snipped into smaller bunches, and mild cheeses. Serve with small bread sticks and cheese crackers.

Pictured on page 61.

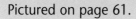

School's Out Backyard Bash

This is the perfect menu for a "cut-loose" backyard barbecue. Invite your child's classmates over to celebrate the end of a long school year and the start of summer.

---

serves 8

Chilling Melon Drinks

Munchies

Bacon-Stuffed Tomatoes

Sesame Steak Skewers

Tangy Yogurt Pops

REPORT CARD

Top Centre: Chilling Melon Drinks, page 66
Centre Left and Centre Right: Munchies, page 66
Centre: Bacon-Stuffed Tomatoes, page 67
Bottom: Sesame Steak Skewers, page 68

Chilling Melon Drinks

Fizzy melon-flavoured beverage. Crisp, cool and refreshing! Pretty pink ice cubes in a clear, sparkling drink.

Coarsely chopped seedless (or seeds removed) watermelon	3 cups	750 mL
White grape juice	1 cup	250 mL
White corn syrup	1/4 cup	60 mL
Raspberry ginger ale (or lemon lime soft drink)	8 cups	2 L

Process watermelon, grape juice and corn syrup in blender, in 2 batches, until smooth. Divide and pour into 3 ice cube trays. Freeze for at least 2 hours until cubes are solid. Makes about 36 cubes.

Place 4 or 5 cubes in each of eight 8 oz. (227 mL) glasses. Fill each glass with ginger ale. Serves 8.

1 serving: 162 Calories; 0.3 g Total Fat (0 g Mono, 0 g Poly, 0 g Sat); 0 mg Cholesterol; 41 g Carbohydrate; trace Fibre; 1 g Protein; 28 mg Sodium

Pictured on page 65.

Munchies

What's a party without chips and cheesies or popcorn? Have some in large bowls.

Combine some favourite treats in bowls, for example, candy, peanuts, broken string licorice, pretzels, raisins, chopped dried fruit, salted sunflower or pumpkin seeds. Then provide small paper cups for children to scoop their own treats.

Arrange a variety of fresh, raw vegetables on serving platter along with bowl of Ranch (or other) dressing for dipping.

Pictured on page 65 and on page 69.

Bacon-Stuffed Tomatoes

Pop-in-your-mouth veggies. Delicious!

Small cherry tomatoes	16	16
Salt	1/4 tsp.	1 mL
Cream cheese, softened	1/3 cup	75 mL
Mayonnaise (or salad dressing)	1 tbsp.	15 mL
Finely chopped fresh chives (or 1/2 tsp., 2 mL, dried)	2 tsp.	10 mL
Bacon slices, cooked crisp and crumbled	7	7
Chopped fresh parsley (or flakes), for garnish		
Bacon slice, cooked and cut into 16 pieces, for garnish	1	1

Remove stems from tomatoes. Remove small slice from opposite end. Scoop out and discard seeds and flesh with small spoon, leaving hollow tomato shell. Sprinkle inside with salt. Turn stem-side up on several layers of paper towel for 30 minutes to drain.

Mash cream cheese and mayonnaise together with fork in small bowl until smooth. Stir in chives.

Add first amount of bacon. Stir until combined. Spoon cream cheese mixture into small freezer bag. Snip 1/2 inch (12 mm) hole from corner of bag. Squeeze 1 1/2 to 2 tsp. (7 to 10 mL) into each tomato shell to fill.

Garnish each with parsley and 1 bacon piece. Chill for at least 3 hours. Makes 16 stuffed tomatoes.

1 stuffed tomato: 43 Calories; 3.9 g Total Fat (1.6 g Mono, 0.5 g Poly, 1.7 g Sat); 8 mg Cholesterol; 1 g Carbohydrate; trace Fibre; 1 g Protein; 102 mg Sodium

Pictured on page 65.

Sesame Steak Skewers

A tender, tasty treat, easy to eat outside.

Flank steak, partially frozen	1 1/2 lbs.	680 g
Bamboo skewers (8 inch, 20 cm, length), soaked in water for 10 minutes	24	24
MARINADE		
Water	1/3 cup	75 mL
Soy sauce	1/3 cup	75 mL
Garlic cloves, halved (or 1/2 tsp., 2 mL, powder)	2	2
Green onions, cut into 4 pieces each	2	2
Brown sugar, packed	2 tbsp.	30 mL
Ketchup (or chili sauce)	2 tbsp.	30 mL
Sesame (or cooking) oil	2 tsp.	10 mL
Sesame seeds	1 tbsp.	15 mL

Slice steak thinly across grain on diagonal. Thread beef, accordion-style, onto skewers, leaving about 2 inches (5 cm) on 1 end as handle. Lay skewers in 9 x 13 inch (22 x 33 cm) glass baking dish.

Marinade: Process first 7 ingredients in blender until smooth. Makes about 1 cup (250 mL) marinade. Pour over skewers. Turn to coat. Cover. Marinate in refrigerator for at least 2 hours, turning several times.

Discard marinade. Preheat gas barbecue to medium. Sprinkle skewers with sesame seeds. Cook on lightly greased grill for about 2 minutes per side until desired doneness. Pile onto platter. Makes 24 skewers.

1 skewer: 57 Calories; 2.9 g Total Fat (1.2 g Mono, 0.3 g Poly, 1.1 g Sat); 12 mg Cholesterol; 1 g Carbohydrate; trace Fibre; 6 g Protein; 146 mg Sodium

Pictured on page 65.

Tangy Yogurt Pops

Sweet, tart and tangy! A cool frozen treat.

Vanilla yogurt	2 cups	500 mL
Frozen concentrated orange juice (or your child's favourite), thawed	3/4 cup	175 mL
White grape juice	1/2 cup	125 mL
Disposable paper drink cups (about 4 oz., 114 mL, size), see Note	8	8
Popsicle sticks	8	8

Beat first 3 ingredients together in medium bowl until well combined.

Divide and pour into 8 disposable cups. Place cups on ungreased baking sheet. Freeze for about 1 1/2 hours until partially frozen. Insert stick into centre of each cup. Freeze for 3 to 4 hours until firm. Makes 8 popsicles.

1 popsicle: 114 Calories; 1.3 g Total Fat (0.4 g Mono, 0.1 g Poly, 0.8 g Sat); 3 mg Cholesterol; 23 g Carbohydrate; trace Fibre; 3 g Protein; 39 mg Sodium

Pictured below.

Note: A popsicle mold may be used instead of drink cups and popsicle sticks.

Top Left and Bottom: Tangy Yogurt Pops, above   Top Right: Munchies, page 66

Soccer Windup

*Celebrate a successful soccer season with these fun,
creative recipes. This menu includes a variety of hearty
finger foods to satisfy a large group of hungry, active kids.*

serves 16 – 20

Keeper Cheese Wedges

Teamed-Up Popcorn Snack

Windup Wings

Caesar Salad

Soccer Ball Cupcakes

Root Beer Floats

Top Centre: Keeper Cheese Wedges, page 72
Top Left: Root Beer Floats, page 75
Centre Right: Windup Wings, page 74
Bottom: Soccer Ball Cupcakes, page 75

Keeper Cheese Wedges

Colourful and tasty, these bacon and cheese-filled quesadillas will satisfy any young athlete's hunger.

Large egg	1	1
Sweet (or regular) chili sauce	1 tbsp.	15 mL
Large flour tortillas (10 inch, 25 cm, diameter)	12	12
Taco sauce	1/4 cup	60 mL
Grated Tex-Mex cheese (or equal amounts of Cheddar and Monterey Jack cheeses)	1 1/2 cups	375 mL
Package of bacon, cooked crisp and crumbled (about 1 1/4 cups, 300 mL)	17 1/2 oz.	500 g
Finely sliced green onion	1/4 cup	60 mL
Finely chopped red (or green) pepper	1/4 cup	60 mL

Combine egg and chili sauce in small bowl. Brush 1 side of 6 tortillas with egg mixture. Set aside.

Spread 2 tsp. (10 mL) taco sauce on 1 side of remaining 6 tortillas.

Divide and sprinkle cheese, bacon, green onion and red pepper in layers over taco sauce, leaving 1/2 inch (12 mm) edge. Place remaining tortillas, egg-side down, over top. Press edges together to seal. Preheat gas barbecue to medium-low. Place 2 or 3 tortillas on greased grill. Grill 2 minutes or until bottom shows grill marks. Flip to cook other side. Repeat with remaining tortillas. Cut each into 8 wedges. Makes 48 wedges.

3 wedges: 204 Calories; 10.4 g Total Fat (4.1 g Mono, 1.5 g Poly, 4.2 g Sat); 32 mg Cholesterol; 18 g Carbohydrate; 1 g Fibre; 9 g Protein; 385 mg Sodium

Pictured on page 71.

Teamed-Up Popcorn Snack

A tasty snack—enough for a crowd. Cheese-flavoured popcorn can be used in place of plain popcorn.

Popped corn (about 1/2 cup, 125 mL, unpopped)	12 cups	3 L
Hard margarine (or butter)	1/2 cup	125 mL
Hot pepper sauce (optional)	1/8 tsp.	0.5 mL
Onion salt	1/2 tsp.	2 mL
Garlic salt	1/2 tsp.	2 mL
Bag of corn chips	8 1/2 oz.	240 g
Bag of Hickory-flavoured (or plain) shoestring potato chips	10 1/2 oz.	300 g

Put popped corn into very large bowl or container.

Heat margarine and hot pepper sauce in small saucepan on medium for about 3 minutes until margarine is melted. Drizzle over popcorn. Toss well to coat.

Sprinkle with onion salt and garlic salt.

Add both chips to popcorn mixture. Toss well to distribute evenly. Makes about 23 cups (5.75 L).

1 cup (250 mL): 175 Calories; 12.1 g Total Fat (4.7 g Mono, 4.4 g Poly, 2.4 g Sat); 0 mg Cholesterol; 16 g Carbohydrate; 2 g Fibre; 2 g Protein; 265 mg Sodium

Pictured below.

Windup Wings

Mildly sweet-and-sour wings that will leave them licking their fingers!

Chicken drumettes (or whole chicken wings, split in half and tips discarded)	3 lbs.	1.4 kg
Seasoned salt	1 tsp.	5 mL
Pepper	1/4 tsp.	1 mL
Brown sugar, packed	1/2 cup	125 mL
All-purpose flour	2 tbsp.	30 mL
Pineapple juice	1/4 cup	60 mL
Lemon juice	2 tbsp.	30 mL
Soy sauce	2 tbsp.	30 mL
Ketchup	3 tbsp.	50 mL

Pat drumettes dry. Arrange in single layer on large baking sheet lined with greased foil. Sprinkle with seasoned salt and pepper. Bake in 400°F (205°C) oven for about 20 minutes until no longer pink inside. Remove from oven. Drain well. Transfer to large bowl.

Combine brown sugar and flour in small saucepan. Add pineapple and lemon juices. Stir until smooth. Add soy sauce and ketchup. Stir. Cook on medium for about 7 minutes, stirring often, until boiling and thickened. Pour over drumettes. Toss until well coated. Cool. Cover. Marinate in refrigerator for up to 24 hours. Preheat gas barbecue to medium-low. Drain and discard marinade. Heat drumettes on greased grill for about 15 minutes, turning often, until heated through and browned. Makes about 36 pieces.

1 piece: 58 Calories; 3 g Total Fat (1.2 g Mono, 0.6 g Poly, 0.8 g Sat); 14 mg Cholesterol; 4 g Carbohydrate; trace Fibre; 4 g Protein; 121 mg Sodium

Pictured on page 71.

FAST WINGS: Barbecue immediately after coating with sauce if there is no time to marinate.

Caesar Salad

Make your favourite Caesar salad recipe in the biggest bowl you have, with lots of croutons and freshly grated Parmesan cheese. Kids will usually eat Caesar salad over any other. Note: One 10 oz. (285 g) bag of Caesar salad mix yields about 3 1/2 cups (875 mL) salad. Buy several bags.

Soccer Ball Cupcakes

A giant soccer ball on green coconut "grass." Fun and easy to make. Everyone gets their own "ball."

Box of white (or chocolate) cake mix (2 layer size)	1	1
Black (or white) cupcake liners	24	24
Container of vanilla frosting	16 oz.	450 g
Black licorice laces (about 2 oz., 57 g), cut into 1 1/4 inch (3 cm) pieces	8	8
Tubes of red (and/or blue) decorating gel (2/3 oz., 19 g, each)	2	2
Drops of green liquid food colouring	8	8
Water	1 1/2 tbsp.	25 mL
Flake coconut	3 cups	750 mL

Prepare cake mix according to package directions. Line muffin cups with paper liners. Fill liners 2/3 full. Bake as directed on package for cupcakes. Cool.

Spread tops of cupcakes with frosting. Arrange licorice pieces on frosting to make pentagon shape.

Write each child's name or initials in centre of pentagon with decorating gel.

Combine food colouring and water in large plastic bag. Add coconut. Shake until evenly tinted. Sprinkle onto parchment (or waxed) paper-lined baking sheet. Bake in 250°F (120°C) oven for about 20 minutes until dry but not browned. Cool. Spread in even layer on large round platter. Arrange cupcakes on top of coconut. Makes 24 cupcakes.

1 cupcake: 227 Calories; 8.7 g Total Fat (2.8 g Mono, 1.4 g Poly, 4.1 g Sat); 0 mg Cholesterol; 37 g Carbohydrate; trace Fibre; 1 g Protein; 193 mg Sodium

Pictured on page 71.

Root Beer Floats

Have several 2 quart (2 L) bottles of root beer chilled and 1 gallon (4 L) of vanilla ice cream. Put 1 scoop of ice cream into each of 16 to 20 large (12 oz., 341 mL) plastic drink cups. Slowly pour root beer over ice cream until foam reaches top of cup. Add straw and long-handled spoon.

Pictured on page 71.

Holiday Sledding Party

A warm, comforting menu that will revive famished kids after a cold day in the snow. These recipes are deliciously attractive—definitely worth coming inside for.

serves 6

Winter Warming Fondue

Hot Fudge Chocolate

Snow-Capped Cookies

Top Right: Winter Warming Fondue, page 78
Centre Left: Hot Fudge Chocolate, page 78
Bottom: Snow-Capped Cookies, page 79

Winter Warming Fondue

A kid-friendly fondue that's subtly flavoured with onion and cheese.

Homogenized milk	3 cups	750 mL
Medium onion, coarsely chopped	1	1
Hard margarine (or butter)	3 tbsp.	50 mL
Garlic clove, minced (or 1/4 tsp., 1 mL, powder)	1	1
All-purpose flour	3 tbsp.	50 mL
Salt	1/4 tsp.	1 mL
Pepper, just a pinch		
Pasteurized cheese loaf (such as Velveeta), cubed	8 oz.	225 g

Combine milk and onion in heavy medium saucepan. Heat on medium until bubbles appear around edge of saucepan. Remove from heat. Cover. Let stand for 15 minutes. Strain milk into medium bowl and set aside. Discard onion.

Melt margarine in same saucepan on medium-low. Add garlic. Heat and stir for 1 minute until garlic is soft and fragrant.

Add next 3 ingredients. Stir for 1 minute until blended. Gradually add milk, stirring constantly, until smooth. Heat and stir on medium until boiling and thickened.

Add cheese. Heat and stir on low until cheese is melted and sauce is smooth. Place in electric fondue pot or heavy saucepan on hot plate on low to keep warm. Makes 3 1/2 cups (875 mL).

1/2 cup (125 mL): 249 Calories; 17.5 g Total Fat (6.9 g Mono, 0.9 g Poly, 8.8 g Sat); 38 mg Cholesterol; 12 g Carbohydrate; trace Fibre; 11 g Protein; 768 mg Sodium

Pictured on page 77.

Suggested Dippers: Steamed broccoli, cauliflower, carrots, snow peas, bread sticks or baguette toasts.

Hot Fudge Chocolate

Heat 6 cups (1.5 L) homogenized milk in heavy medium saucepan until bubbles appear around edge of saucepan. Add 1 cup (250 mL) chocolate fudge ice cream topping. Heat and stir until hot and well combined. Divide among six 12 oz. (341 mL) mugs. Top each with 10 to 12 coloured miniature marshmallows. Serves 6.

Pictured on page 77.

Snow-Capped Cookies

Frosted cookies with a cap of snowy coconut.

Large egg	1	1
Brown sugar, packed	2/3 cup	150 mL
All-purpose flour (3/4 cup, 175 mL, plus 2 tbsp., 30 mL)	7/8 cup	200 mL
Baking powder	3/4 tsp.	4 mL
Baking soda	1/4 tsp.	1 mL
Hard margarine (or butter), melted	1/4 cup	60 mL
Pecan pieces, toasted (see Note)	1/2 cup	125 mL
White chocolate chips	1/2 cup	125 mL
Commercial vanilla frosting	2/3 cup	150 mL
Medium sweetened coconut	1/2 cup	125 mL

Beat egg and brown sugar in medium bowl until pale.

Combine flour, baking powder and baking soda in small bowl. Add 1/2 to egg mixture. Stir.

Add margarine. Combine well. Add remaining flour mixture. Stir until no dry flour remains.

Add pecans and chocolate chips. Combine well. Cover. Chill for 1 to 2 hours. Roll into balls, using about 1 tbsp. (15 mL) for each. Arrange 2 inches (5 cm) apart on greased cookie sheets. Bake in 375°F (190°C) oven for 8 to 10 minutes until lightly browned. Let stand on cookie sheets for 5 minutes before removing to wire racks to cool.

Spread about 1 tsp. (5 mL) frosting on each cooled cookie. Immediately sprinkle with coconut before frosting sets. Makes about 30 cookies.

1 cookie: 124 Calories; 6.1 g Total Fat (3.1 g Mono, 0.8 g Poly, 1.9 g Sat); 8 mg Cholesterol; 17 g Carbohydrate; trace Fibre; 1 g Protein; 57 mg Sodium

Pictured on page 77.

Note: To toast pecans, place in single layer on ungreased shallow pan. Bake in 350°F (175°C) oven for 5 to 10 minutes, stirring or shaking often, until desired doneness.

Spring Break Bake

Enjoy Spring Break with some special treats. Get the kids involved when making this menu. They'll have lots of fun decorating the desserts. Any extras can be given as party favours.

serves 4

Frosty Peach Drink

Open-Faced Salmon Buns

Rabbit Food

Easter Hats

Cookie Bouquets

Centre Left and Top Right: Frosty Peach Drink, page 82
Centre Right: Easter Hats, page 83
Centre: Rabbit Food, page 83
Bottom: Open-Faced Salmon Buns, page 82

Frosty Peach Drink

Peach, orange and vanilla make this creamy drink irresistible.

Can of sliced peaches (with syrup), chilled	14 oz.	398 mL
Orange juice	1 cup	250 mL
Vanilla ice cream	2 cups	500 mL

Process peaches with syrup and orange juice in blender until smooth.

Add ice cream. Process for several seconds until smooth. Divide among four 10 oz. (284 mL) glasses. Serves 4.

1 serving: 213 Calories; 7.8 g Total Fat (2.3 g Mono, 0.3 g Poly, 4.8 g Sat); 31 mg Cholesterol; 35 g Carbohydrate; trace Fibre; 3 g Protein; 62 mg Sodium

Pictured on page 81.

Open-Faced Salmon Buns

A hearty sandwich to fill the empty stomachs of hard-working bakers.

Can of red salmon, drained, skin and round bones removed	7 1/2 oz.	213 g
Grated medium Cheddar cheese	1/2 cup	250 mL
Salad dressing (or mayonnaise)	1/4 cup	60 mL
Grated onion	1 tsp.	5 mL
Lemon juice	1/2 tsp.	2 mL
Parsley flakes	1/2 tsp.	2 mL
Pepper, just a pinch		
Hard margarine (or butter), softened	2 tbsp.	30 mL
Large hot dog buns (or hamburger buns), split	2	2

Mash first 7 ingredients together with fork in small bowl.

Spread margarine on cut sides of bun halves. Divide and spread salmon mixture over margarine. Arrange bun halves on ungreased baking sheet. Broil on top rack in oven until heated through and browned. Makes 4 bun halves.

1 bun half: 393 Calories; 29.5 g Total Fat (13.6 g Mono, 5 g Poly, 9.5 g Sat); 48 mg Cholesterol; 13 g Carbohydrate; trace Fibre; 18 g Protein; 679 mg Sodium

Pictured on page 81.

OPEN-FACED TUNA BUNS: Omit salmon. Use 6 1/2 oz. (184 g) can of tuna.

Fill inside ribs of celery hearts with process cheese spread or peanut butter. Dot with raisins, dried blueberries or drained pineapple tidbits.

Pictured on page 81.

Easter Hats

Sweet cookie "hats" with decorative garnishes.

Flat round cookies (such as digestive biscuits or Dare sugar cookies)	16	16
Jelly preserves (your child's favourite flavour)	4 tsp.	20 mL
Large marshmallows, cut in half crosswise	8	8
Pastel-coloured melting wafers (see Note)	2 1/2 cups	625 mL
DECORATIONS		
Glazed cherries, cut in half	8	8
Dried fruit pieces (such as pineapple, papaya, lemon or apricot)	8	8
Pastel-coloured candy sprinkles		

Lay cookies on work surface. Spread 1/8 tsp. (0.5 mL) jelly on cut side of each marshmallow. Lightly press onto centre of each cookie.

Melt wafers in small saucepan on low, stirring constantly, until almost melted. Remove from heat. Stir until smooth. Arrange cookies on wire rack over waxed paper-lined baking sheet. Spoon and spread about 4 tsp. (20 mL) melted wafers over each marshmallow and cookie, allowing excess to drip onto waxed paper.

Before coating dries, decorate with 1 cherry half and 1 fruit piece, trimmed to look like a feather or flower, on side of each marshmallow. Top with sprinkles. Makes 16 hats.

1 hat: 182 Calories; 3.2 g Total Fat (1.8 g Mono, 0.4 g Poly, 0.8 g Sat); 8 mg Cholesterol; 39 g Carbohydrate; trace Fibre; 1 g Protein; 66 mg Sodium

Pictured on page 81.

Note: To use several different colours of melting wafers, melt 1/2 cup (125 mL) amounts in separate small heatproof dishes set in hot water in deep electric frying pan on lowest heat. Stir frequently until smooth.

Cookie Bouquets

Flower cookies served on a "stem" are perfect for a spring party.

Shortening (such as Crisco), softened	1/2 cup	125 mL
Granulated sugar	1/2 cup	125 mL
Package of strawberry (or raspberry) flavoured jelly powder (gelatin)	3 oz.	85 g
Large eggs	2	2
All-purpose flour	2 1/2 cups	625 mL
Baking powder	2 tsp.	10 mL
Salt	1/2 tsp.	2 mL
Egg whites, fork-beaten	2	2
Coloured sanding (decorating) sugars (or sprinkles), in various colours		
Lollipop sticks (5 inch, 12.5 cm, length), see Note	14	14
Styrofoam cups (8 oz., 227 mL, size) or foam core for base of cups (optional)	4	4
Plastic pots (12 oz., 341 mL, size), optional	4	4
Marbles (or other weights), optional		
Chocolate wafer crumbs (optional)	2 cups	500 mL

Beat shortening, sugar and jelly powder in large bowl until light and creamy. Beat in eggs, 1 at a time, until well blended.

Combine flour, baking powder and salt in medium bowl. Add, 1/2 cup (125 mL) at a time, to shortening mixture, mixing well after each addition. Divide dough into 4 portions. Roll out 1 portion on lightly floured surface to 1/4 inch (6 mm) thickness. Let children cut dough into shapes with lightly floured 3 to 4 inch (7.5 to 10 cm) flower-shaped cookie cutters. Repeat with remaining dough.

Brush cookie surface with egg white. Let children sprinkle coloured sugars on top. Push lollipop stick 1 to 1 1/2 inches (2.5 to 3.8 cm) into bottom edge of flower shape to make stem. Place "flowers" on greased cookie sheets. Bake in 375°F (190°C) oven for 8 to 10 minutes until edges are golden. Let stand on cookie sheets for 5 minutes before removing to wire rack to cool completely.

(continued on next page)

Cut styrofoam cups to fit upside-down inside pots. Fill cut styrofoam cups with marbles. Invert pot onto filled cup. Invert pot to stand upright. Top with cookie crumbs to resemble dirt. Stand about 3 "flowers" into cups, pushing down through styrofoam 1 to 1 1/2 inches (2.5 to 3.8 cm) to hold upright. Makes about 14 cookies, depending on size of cookie cutters.

1 cookie: 221 Calories; 8.7 g Total Fat (3.6 g Mono, 1.8 g Poly, 2.3 g Sat); 31 mg Cholesterol; 31 g Carbohydrate; trace Fibre; 4 g Protein; 170 mg Sodium

Pictured below and on back cover.

Note: Lollipop sticks are available at craft or candy-making stores.

Tropical Winter Break

Lose yourself in the tropics. Get the kids to come dressed in colourful Hawaiian shirts—they'll practically feel the sun and ocean breeze.

serves 8

Coconut Quenchers

Seafood Basket

Vegetable Cheese Dip

Stowaway Veggies

Celery Palm Trees

Glazed Pineapple Rings

Top: Coconut Quenchers, page 88
Centre Left: Vegetable Cheese Dip, page 89, with Celery Palm Trees, page 90
Bottom: Seafood Basket, page 88, with Stowaway Veggies, page 89

Coconut Quenchers

Creamy tropical beverage full of pineapple, banana, orange and coconut flavours.

Pineapple juice	4 cups	1 L
Orange juice	2 cups	500 mL
Can of coconut milk (see Note)	14 oz.	398 mL
Frozen medium bananas, cut up	2	2
Coconut flavouring (optional)	1/2 tsp.	2 mL
Cocktail umbrellas, for garnish	8	8
Can of pineapple chunks, drained (for garnish)	14 oz.	398 mL

Process first 5 ingredients in blender, in 2 batches, until smooth. Makes 9 cups (2.25 L). Divide and pour into eight 10 oz. (284 mL) glasses.

Decorate with umbrellas and pineapple chunks. Serves 8.

1 serving: 223 Calories; 10.5 g Total Fat (0.5 g Mono, 0.2 g Poly, 9.1 g Sat); 0 mg Cholesterol; 33 g Carbohydrate; 1 g Fibre; 2 g Protein; 8 mg Sodium

Pictured on page 87.

Note: If you can't find coconut milk, use 1 2/3 cups (400 mL) homogenized milk and add 1/2 tsp. (2 mL) coconut flavouring.

Seafood Basket

An individual meal for each child. Mild fish with chips and dip.

Large eggs	2	2
Fine dry bread crumbs	1 cup	250 mL
Finely grated fresh Parmesan cheese	1/2 cup	125 mL
Halibut fillets (or other thick, firm white fish), cut into 1 1/2 inch (3.8 cm) strips	1 1/4 lbs.	560 g
Bag of frozen french fries	2 1/8 lbs.	1 kg
Mayonnaise (or salad dressing)	2/3 cup	150 mL
Ketchup	2/3 cup	150 mL

(continued on next page)

Beat eggs in shallow dish. Combine bread crumbs and Parmesan cheese in separate shallow dish.

Dip each fish piece into egg. Press into bread crumb mixture to coat completely. Place on baking sheet. Cover. Chill for at least 1 hour or overnight. Arrange fish in single layer on separate greased baking sheet. Spray generously with cooking spray. Bake in 375°F (190°C) oven for about 15 minutes until fish is golden and flakes easily when tested with fork. Makes about 48 pieces.

Spread french fries on greased baking sheets. Cook, according to package directions, until golden and crispy.

Combine mayonnaise and ketchup in small bowl. Divide and spoon into small individual bowls or disposable cups. Place in baskets with fries and fish pieces. Serves 8.

1 serving: 502 Calories; 23.2 g Total Fat (12.2 g Mono, 5.2 g Poly, 4 g Sat); 87 mg Cholesterol; 50 g Carbohydrate; 3 g Fibre; 24 g Protein; 709 mg Sodium

Pictured on page 87.

Variation: Fish can be deep-fried in hot (375°F, 190°C) cooking oil for about 3 minutes until golden and cooked through. Remove to paper towel to drain.

Vegetable Cheese Dip

Creamy cheese dip perfect for vegetables and crackers.

Process cheese spread (such as Cheez Whiz)	1/2 cup	125 mL
Thick plain yogurt (not fat-free)	1/2 cup	125 mL
Mayonnaise (not salad dressing)	1/4 cup	60 mL
Grated carrot	2 tbsp.	30 mL
Minced green onion (or fresh chives)	1 tbsp.	15 mL
Milk	1 – 2 tsp.	5 – 10 mL
Sun-dried tomato pesto	1 tsp.	5 mL

Process all 7 ingredients in blender or food processor, scraping down sides if necessary, until almost smooth. Makes 1 2/3 cups (400 mL) dip.

2 tbsp. (30 mL): 66 Calories; 5.6 g Total Fat (2.5 g Mono, 1.2 g Poly, 1.7 g Sat); 8 mg Cholesterol; 2 g Carbohydrate; trace Fibre; 2 g Protein; 186 mg Sodium

Pictured on page 87.

Glazed Pineapple Rings

Candied pineapple rings under vanilla ice cream with a cherry on top. A sundae-type dessert sure to cool the kids from the hot sun.

Hard margarine (or butter)	1/4 cup	60 mL
Granulated sugar	1 cup	250 mL
Cans of pineapple slices (14 oz., 398 mL, each), drained (see Note)	2	2
Small scoops of vanilla ice cream	8	8
Maraschino cherries, with stems	8	8

Melt margarine in shallow microwave-safe dish.

Put sugar into separate shallow dish. Dip each pineapple slice into margarine, and then into sugar until well coated. Arrange pineapple slices in single layer on greased baking sheet. Bake in 475°F (240°C) oven for 20 minutes until bottoms are browned and glazed. Turn over. Bake for 5 minutes to brown other side. Immediately remove to separate greased waxed paper-lined baking sheet to cool.

Stack 2 pineapple slices on each of 8 plates. Place scoop of ice cream in centre of each stack. Top with maraschino cherry. Serves 8.

1 serving: 335 Calories; 13.9 g Total Fat (6.2 g Mono, 0.9 g Poly, 6 g Sat); 31 mg Cholesterol; 53 g Carbohydrate; trace Fibre; 3 g Protein; 128 mg Sodium

Pictured on page 91.

Note: To use fresh pineapple instead of canned slices, peel and core fresh pineapple. Cut into crosswise slices, about 3/4 to 1 inch (2 to 2.5 cm) thick. Allow 1 slice per child. Coat in margarine and sugar and bake as for canned slices above.

Stowaway Veggies

Score unpeeled English cucumber with fork. Cut into thin wedges. Add to seafood basket with cherry tomatoes.

Pictured on page 87.

Celery Palm Trees

Trim ends from celery ribs. Cut into 3 inch (7.5 cm) pieces. Cut each piece in half lengthwise. Make several lengthwise cuts almost to middle of celery. Put into ice water. Chill until edges curl, resembling palm trees.

Pictured on page 87.

Victorian Tea Party

*Little girls are sure to love these dainty treats.
Let them dine like royalty! Make these fancy
items ahead for a quaint afternoon tea party.*

serves 6

Fancy Pinwheels

Pinkies Up Sandwiches

A Cup Of Tea

Heart Cookies

Flower Cupcakes

Chocolate-Dipped Strawberries

Top Right: Heart Cookies, page 96
Centre and Bottom Right: Flower Cupcakes, page 97
Centre and Bottom Right: Chocolate-Dipped Strawberries, page 97
Bottom Left: Fancy Pinwheels, page 94

Fancy Pinwheels

Thick cream cheese and cranberry jelly combine well with turkey in these pretty and delicious spirals.

Slices of white sandwich bread, crusts removed	6	6
Spreadable cream cheese	1/2 cup	125 mL
Cranberry jelly	3 tbsp.	50 mL
Baby spinach leaves, stems removed, lightly packed	1/4 cup	60 mL
Slices of deli turkey breast (about 3 1/4 oz., 92 g, total)	6	6

Flatten each bread slice slightly with rolling pin. Cover with damp tea towel to keep from drying out.

Combine cream cheese and cranberry jelly in small bowl. Divide and spread on 1 side of each bread slice.

Arrange spinach in even layer over cheese mixture. Lay turkey slice on spinach, leaving about 1/2 inch (12 mm) uncovered at top of bread. Roll up, jelly roll-style, starting at bottom of bread slice. Wrap each roll tightly in plastic wrap. Chill for at least 1 hour or overnight. Cut each roll into 4 slices for a total of 24 pinwheels.

1 pinwheel: 44 Calories; 2.1 g Total Fat (0.6 g Mono, 0.1 g Poly, 1.2 g Sat); 7 mg Cholesterol; 5 g Carbohydrate; trace Fibre; 2 g Protein; 62 mg Sodium

Pictured on page 93.

Pinkies Up Sandwiches

Delightful, little triangular egg salad sandwiches made with white and brown bread.

FILLING		
Large hard-cooked eggs, peeled	4	4
Finely chopped celery	3 tbsp.	50 mL
Mayonnaise (or salad dressing)	3 tbsp.	50 mL
Finely chopped green onion (optional)	1 tbsp.	15 mL
Salt, just a pinch		

(continued on next page)

Hard margarine (or butter), softened	3 tbsp.	50 mL
Slices of white sandwich bread, crusts removed	6	6
Slices of whole wheat sandwich bread, crusts removed	6	6

Filling: Mash eggs with fork in medium bowl.

Add next 4 ingredients. Mix well. Makes about 1 cup (250 mL) filling.

Spread margarine on 1 side of each bread slice. Divide and spread egg mixture over margarine on each slice of white bread. Top with whole wheat slices, margarine-side down. Cut each sandwich into 4 triangles. Arrange upright on serving platter. Makes 24 sandwiches.

1 sandwich: 73 Calories; 4.3 g Total Fat (2.3 g Mono, 0.9 g Poly, 0.8 g Sat); 37 mg Cholesterol; 7 g Carbohydrate; trace Fibre; 2 g Protein; 108 mg Sodium

Pictured below.

A Cup Of Tea

Use herbal teas, especially when a specific colour is desired, because they are caffeine free.

Pictured below.

Heart Cookies

Sweet strawberry and marshmallow filling between soft, heart-shaped cookies.
These can be made ahead of time and frozen.

Hard margarine (or butter), softened	1/2 cup	125 mL
Granulated sugar	1/3 cup	75 mL
Large egg	1	1
Liquid honey	2 tbsp.	30 mL
Vanilla	1/2 tsp.	2 mL
All-purpose flour	1 2/3 cups	400 mL
STRAWBERRY FILLING		
Strawberry jam	1/2 cup	125 mL
Large marshmallows, cut into quarters	8	8

Icing (confectioner's) sugar, for dusting

Beat margarine and sugar in medium bowl for about 5 minutes until light
and creamy.

Add next 3 ingredients. Beat until well combined.

Mix in flour. Gently knead dough on lightly floured surface until smooth. Shape
into flattened ball. Wrap in plastic wrap. Chill for 30 minutes. Roll out dough on
lightly floured surface to 1/8 to 1/4 inch (3 to 6 mm) thickness. Cut out shapes
with lightly floured heart-shaped cookie cutter (about 2 inch, 5 cm, diameter).
Place on lightly greased cookie sheets about 1/2 inch (12 mm) apart. Repeat
with dough scraps. Bake in 350°F (175°C) oven for 10 to 12 minutes until firm
and edges are golden. Let stand on cookie sheets for 10 minutes before
removing to wire racks to cool. Makes about 24 cookies.

Strawberry Filling: Heat jam and marshmallows in small saucepan for about
4 minutes, stirring constantly, until marshmallows are melted. Turn into small
bowl. Let stand for about 45 minutes, stirring occasionally, until thickened and
consistency of smooth peanut butter.

Lay 12 cookies, bottom-side up, on work surface. Spread each with about 2 tsp.
(10 mL) filling. Top with remaining cookies, right-side up. Dust with icing sugar.
Makes about 12 sandwich cookies.

1 sandwich cookie: 228 Calories; 8.7 g Total Fat (5.4 g Mono, 0.9 g Poly, 1.8 g Sat); 18 mg Cholesterol;
36 g Carbohydrate; trace Fibre; 3 g Protein; 108 mg Sodium

Pictured on page 93.

Flower Cupcakes

Small cakes with dainty marshmallow flowers. Pink and pretty.

Package of yellow cake mix (1 layer size), or your child's favourite flavour	1	1
ICING		
Icing (confectioner's) sugar	1 1/2 cups	375 mL
Hard margarine (or butter), melted	2 tbsp.	30 mL
Milk	1 tbsp.	15 mL
Drop of red liquid food colouring	1	1
Small white (or coloured) marshmallows	1 cup	250 mL
Silver dragées (tiny candy balls)	3 tbsp.	50 mL

Prepare cake mix according to package directions. Grease muffin cups with cooking spray or line with pink and/or white paper liners. Fill cups 2/3 full. Bake in 350°F (175°C) oven for 15 to 20 minutes until wooden pick inserted in centre of cupcake comes out clean. Let stand in pan for 10 minutes before removing to wire rack to cool.

Icing: Combine first 4 ingredients in small bowl. Stir, adding up to 1 tbsp. (15 mL) more milk if necessary, until spreadable consistency. Makes about 3/4 cup (175 mL) icing. Ice top of each cupcake.

Cut marshmallows horizontally in half. Pinch ends to create petal shape. Arrange 6 marshmallow pieces in flower pattern on icing. Place silver dragées in centre of each flower. Makes 12 cupcakes.

1 cupcake: 288 Calories; 6.9 g Total Fat (3.3 g Mono, 2 g Poly, 1.1 g Sat); 1 mg Cholesterol; 55 g Carbohydrate; 0 g Fibre; 2 g Protein; 306 mg Sodium

Pictured on page 93.

Chocolate-Dipped Strawberries

Heat 4 white chocolate baking squares (1 oz., 28 g, each), cut up, in heavy small saucepan on low, stirring often, until chocolate is almost melted. Remove from heat. Stir until smooth. Spoon into small container. Dip 12 clean, dry strawberries, with hull on, 1 at a time, halfway into chocolate. Place on waxed paper (or foil) lined baking sheet. Let stand for about 45 minutes until chocolate is set.

Pictured on page 93.

Hockey Game Sleepover

*Score big points with this fun combination of
foods. Great to munch on while watching the
big game or after playing one of your own.*

serves 4

Crispy Trail Mix

Face-Off Pizzas

Chicken Nuggets

Ice Cream Sandwich Pucks

Top: Ice Cream Sandwich Pucks, page 101
Centre Left: Chicken Nuggets, page 101
Centre Right: Crispy Trail Mix, page 100
Bottom: Face-Off Pizzas, page 100

Crispy Trail Mix

Sweet, salty and crunchy. A touch of spice in each bite.

Egg white (large)	1	1
Granulated sugar	2/3 cup	150 mL
Ground nutmeg	1/4 tsp.	1 mL
Salt	1/4 tsp.	1 mL
Mini pretzel twists (about 2 oz., 57 g)	2 cups	500 mL
Whole almonds	1 cup	250 mL
Pecan halves	1 cup	250 mL
Dried cranberries	1 cup	250 mL

Combine first 4 ingredients with whisk in large bowl until foamy.

Add remaining 4 ingredients. Stir to coat. Spread on greased baking sheet. Bake in 300°F (150°C) oven for about 45 minutes, turning every 15 minutes, until dry. Let stand on baking sheet until cool. Makes 6 cups (1.5 L).

1 cup (250 mL): 437 Calories; 26.4 g Total Fat (16.6 g Mono, 6 g Poly, 2.4 g Sat); 0 mg Cholesterol; 48 g Carbohydrate; 6 g Fibre; 8 g Protein; 275 mg Sodium

Pictured on page 99.

Face-Off Pizzas

Colourful, crispy wedges of pizza. A great snack while watching the big game!

Prebaked pizza crusts (such as Boboli), about 6 inch (15 cm) diameter	4	4
Pizza sauce	1/2 cup	125 mL
Grated pizza cheese (or 1/4 cup, 60 mL, each of Cheddar and part-skim mozzarella cheese)	1/2 cup	125 mL
Small tomatoes, thinly sliced	2	2
Slices of salami, cut into thin strips	8	8
Thinly sliced red pepper	1/2 cup	125 mL
Grated pizza cheese (or 2/3 cup, 150 mL, each of Cheddar and part-skim mozzarella cheese)	1 1/3 cups	325 mL

(continued on next page)

Place pizza crusts on large greased baking sheet. Spread each with 2 tbsp. (30 mL) pizza sauce. Divide and sprinkle first amount of cheese over sauce.

Layer next 4 ingredients, in order given, on each pizza. Bake on bottom rack in 450°F (230°C) oven for about 12 minutes until crust is golden and cheese is melted. Cut each into 4 wedges. Serves 4.

1 serving: 526 Calories; 27.6 g Total Fat (9.1 g Mono, 1.8 g Poly, 13.2 g Sat); 78 mg Cholesterol; 43 g Carbohydrate; 1 g Fibre; 26 g Protein; 1236 mg Sodium

Pictured on page 99.

Chicken Nuggets

Prepare commercial chicken nuggets according to package directions. Allow 6 nuggets per person. Serve with equal amounts of sour cream and salsa mixed for dipping.

Pictured on page 99.

Ice Cream Sandwich Pucks

Kids will satisfy their chocolate craving with these ice-cold pucks. Recipe is easy to double, triple or quadruple, so some can always be available for snacking!

Chocolate ice cream, softened	1 1/3 cups	325 mL
Chocolate wafers	8	8
Chocolate sprinkles	1/3 cup	75 mL

Measure about 1/3 cup (75 mL) ice cream onto 1 wafer. Place another wafer on ice cream. Press down slightly and smooth side with spatula.

Put chocolate sprinkles into shallow dish. Coat side of sandwich with sprinkles in thick layer. Place on baking sheet. Freeze. Repeat, making 3 more sandwiches. Freeze for at least 4 hours until firm. Wrap each sandwich in plastic wrap. Keep frozen until ready to eat. Makes 4 ice cream sandwiches.

1 ice cream sandwich: 228 Calories; 11.3 g Total Fat (3.9 g Mono, 0.6 g Poly, 6.3 g Sat); 19 mg Cholesterol; 31 g Carbohydrate; trace Fibre; 4 g Protein; 117 mg Sodium

Pictured on page 99.

Pillow Party

Encourage good dreams and happy thoughts before bed with this sleepover menu. After enjoying these delicious snacks and tempting treats, kids will hopefully go to bed calm and satisfied.

serves 4

Sandman Sandwiches

Sour Cream And Chive Muffins

Peanut Banana Wraps

Star Gazers' Sundaes

Bedtime Snack

Milky Way Shakes

Top Left: Milky Way Shakes, page 106
Top Right: Sandman Sandwiches, page 104
Bottom Centre: Peanut Banana Wraps, page 105, with Bedtime Snack, page 106

Sandman Sandwiches

Fun shapes of bread with colourful sprinkles. Sweet, buttery and crunchy!

Butter, softened (tastes best)	3 tbsp.	50 mL
Slices of white bread, crusts removed	8	8
Small round coloured sprinkles	1/4 cup	60 mL

Generously butter 1 side of each bread slice. Cut out 8 shapes from bread slices using star and moon-shaped cookie cutters.

Pour sprinkles into small shallow dish. Press shapes, buttered side down, into sprinkles. Makes 8 pieces.

1 piece: 117 Calories; 5.1 g Total Fat (1.6 g Mono, 0.3 g Poly, 2.9 g Sat); 12 mg Cholesterol; 16 g Carbohydrate; trace Fibre; 2 g Protein; 155 mg Sodium

Pictured on page 103.

Sour Cream And Chive Muffins

Mini-muffins with cheese and bacon. Serve with herb-flavoured cream cheese.

All-purpose flour	1 cup	250 mL
Baking powder	2 tsp.	10 mL
Grated medium Cheddar cheese	1/3 cup	75 mL
Chopped fresh chives	1 1/2 tbsp.	25 mL
Bacon slices, cooked crisp and crumbled	3	3
Milk	6 tbsp.	100 mL
Sour cream	2 1/2 tbsp.	37 mL
Cooking oil	1/4 cup	60 mL
Egg yolk (large), fork-beaten (see Note)	1	1

Combine flour and baking powder in large bowl.

Add next 3 ingredients. Mix well.

Combine remaining 4 ingredients in small bowl. Add to flour mixture. Stir until just moistened. Do not overmix. Divide batter among 12 greased mini-muffin cups. Bake in 375°F (190°C) oven for about 20 minutes until wooden pick inserted in centre of muffin comes out clean. Let stand in pan for 5 minutes before removing to wire rack to cool. Makes 12 mini-muffins.

(continued on next page)

1 mini-muffin: 119 Calories; 7.8 g Total Fat (3.9 g Mono, 1.7 g Poly, 1.8 g Sat); 24 mg Cholesterol; 9 g Carbohydrate; trace Fibre; 3 g Protein; 114 mg Sodium

Pictured below.

Note: Make 24 mini-muffins by doubling all ingredients, but using 1 whole egg instead of just the yolk.

Peanut Banana Wraps

A comforting nighttime snack. A bit messy, so be sure to have napkins on hand!

Smooth peanut butter	1/3 cup	75 mL
Medium flour tortillas	2	2
(about 8 inch, 20 cm, diameter)		
Small bananas, sliced	2	2
Liquid honey (optional)	1 1/2 tbsp.	25 mL

Spread peanut butter evenly on each tortilla, leaving 1 inch (2.5 cm) edge.

Arrange banana slices, overlapping, down centre of peanut butter. Drizzle with honey. Fold in sides. Roll up from bottom to enclose bananas securely. Cut in half diagonally. Makes 4 halves.

1 half: 233 Calories; 13 g Total Fat (6 g Mono, 3.7 g Poly, 2.6 g Sat); 0 mg Cholesterol; 25 g Carbohydrate; 3 g Fibre; 8 g Protein; 190 mg Sodium

Pictured on page 103.

Star Gazers' Sundae

A delicious ice cream treat. Yum!

WARM FUDGE SAUCE

Whipping cream	1/3 cup	75 mL
Semi-sweet chocolate baking squares (1 oz., 28 g, each), chopped	2	2
Large white marshmallows, halved	8	8
Scoops of strawberry ice cream	8	8
Frozen whipped topping, thawed	3/4 cup	175 mL
Star-shaped sprinkles	2 tsp.	10 mL
Maraschino cherries (with stems)	4	4

Warm Fudge Sauce: Combine whipping cream, chocolate and marshmallows in small saucepan. Heat and stir on medium-low for about 15 minutes until almost melted. Remove from heat. Stir until smooth. Pour into small heatproof pitcher. Makes 3/4 cup (175 mL) sauce.

Place 2 scoops of ice cream in each of 4 sundae glasses. Drizzle with sauce.

Top ice cream in each glass with whipped topping, sprinkles and 1 cherry. Serve immediately. Makes 4 sundaes.

1 sundae: 505 Calories; 26.4 g Total Fat (3.6 g Mono, 0.4 g Poly, 9.9 g Sat); 65 mg Cholesterol; 67 g Carbohydrate; trace Fibre; 6 g Protein; 104 mg Sodium

Pictured on page 107.

Bedtime Snack

Arrange slices of red apples (with peel), small bunches of grapes, and slices of cheese and crackers on a serving platter.

Pictured on page 103.

Milky Way Shakes

Process 2 cups (500 mL) vanilla ice cream, 2 cups (250 mL) milk and 1/3 cup (75 ml) caramel sauce in blender until smooth. Serves 4.

Pictured on page 103.

Snacks & Games Night

Irresistible snack foods that will have everyone coming back for more. This is a fantastic party idea for a cold evening. Break out the cards and board games and enjoy!

serves 4

Pair-O-Dice Spritzer

Sweet And Salty Popcorn

Coconut Chicken Lollipops

Grilled Ham And Pineapple Sandwiches

Domino Brownies

Top Left: Coconut Chicken Lollipops with Dipping Sauce, page 111
Top Right: Pair-O-Dice Spritzer, page 110
Centre Left: Sweet And Salty Popcorn, page 110
Bottom: Grilled Ham And Pineapple Sandwiches, page 112

Pair-O-Dice Spritzer

A refreshing beverage to cool the competitive rush.

Crushed ice	2 cups	500 mL
Pineapple juice	1 cup	250 mL
Lemon lime soft drink	1 cup	250 mL
Grenadine syrup (or syrup from jar of maraschino cherries)	4 tsp.	20 mL

Divide ice among four 8 oz. (227 mL) clear glasses. Pour 1/4 cup (60 mL) each pineapple juice and soft drink into each glass. Pour 1 tsp. (5 mL) grenadine syrup down inside edge of each glass. Do not stir. Serves 4.

1 serving: 82 Calories; 0.1 g Total Fat (0 g Mono, 0 g Poly, 0 g Sat); 0 mg Cholesterol; 21 g Carbohydrate; trace Fibre; 0 g Protein; 16 mg Sodium

Pictured on page 109.

Sweet And Salty Popcorn

Clear, sweet candy coating on small clusters of popcorn. Easy make-ahead recipe.

Granulated sugar	2/3 cup	150 mL
Light corn syrup	2/3 cup	150 mL
Salt	3/4 tsp.	4 mL
Popped corn (about 1/3 cup, 75 mL, unpopped)	8 cups	2 L

Heat and stir sugar, syrup and salt in large pot or Dutch oven on medium for about 5 minutes until hot and sugar is dissolved.

Add popped corn. Stir until well coated and sticky. Spread on greased baking sheet in single layer. Bake in 250°F (120°C) oven for about 1 hour, turning and mixing twice, until dry. Let stand on baking sheet until completely cooled. Break apart into small clusters. Makes about 8 cups (2 L).

1 cup (250 mL): 182 Calories; 0.4 g Total Fat (0.1 g Mono, 0.2 g Poly, 0.1 g Sat); 0 mg Cholesterol; 46 g Carbohydrate; 1 g Fibre; 1 g Protein; 258 mg Sodium

Pictured on page 109.

Coconut Chicken Lollipops

Large chicken chunks with a crunchy coating and a sweet sauce for dipping.

DIPPING SAUCE		
Apricot jam	1/2 cup	125 mL
Dijon mustard	1 tbsp.	15 mL
Lemon (or lime) juice	1 tbsp.	15 mL
Ground ginger	1/4 tsp.	1 mL
COCONUT CHICKEN LOLLIPOPS		
Large egg	1	1
Salt	1/4 tsp.	1 mL
Medium unsweetened coconut	1/2 cup	125 mL
Fine dry bread crumbs	1/2 cup	125 mL
Boneless, skinless chicken breast halves, cut into quarters	3/4 lb.	340 g
Cooking oil, for deep-frying	4 cups	1 L
Lollipop sticks (5 inch, 2.5 cm, length), see Note	12	12

Dipping Sauce: Combine all 4 ingredients in small saucepan. Heat and stir on medium-low for about 5 minutes until jam is warmed. Press through sieve into small dish. Makes about 1/2 cup (125 mL) sauce.

Coconut Chicken Lollipops: Combine egg and salt in shallow dish.

Combine coconut and bread crumbs in separate shallow dish.

Dip chicken into egg, then press into coconut mixture to coat.

Cook chicken in hot 375°F (190°C) cooking oil in medium saucepan, in 2 batches, for about 4 minutes until no longer pink inside. Remove to paper towel to drain.

Poke holes into chicken pieces. Insert lollipop sticks into chicken. Serve with sauce. Makes 12 skewers.

1 skewer: 159 Calories; 8.4 g Total Fat (3.2 g Mono, 1.7 g Poly, 2.9 g Sat); 34 mg Cholesterol; 14 g Carbohydrate; trace Fibre; 8 g Protein; 120 mg Sodium

Pictured on page 109.

Note: Lollipop sticks are available at craft or candy-making stores.

Grilled Ham And Pineapple Sandwiches

Sweet pineapple, cheese and ham—a delicious combination.

Slices of white (or whole wheat) bread	8	8
Hard margarine (or butter), softened	2 tbsp.	30 mL
Process Cheddar cheese slices	4	4
Slices of canned pineapple, blotted dry with paper towel	4	4
Deli ham slices (about 4 oz., 113 g, total)	4	4

Spread 4 slices of bread with 1/2 of margarine.

Layer with cheese, pineapple and ham, in order given, on unbuttered side of bread. Spread remaining bread slices with remaining margarine. Place bread, margarine-side up, over ham. Preheat two-sided grill or sandwich maker for 5 minutes. Place sandwiches on grill. Close lid. Cook for 3 to 5 minutes until crisp and golden. Cut each sandwich into triangles to serve. Makes 4 whole sandwiches.

1 whole sandwich: 371 Calories; 20.3 g Total Fat (8.4 g Mono, 2.3 g Poly, 8.3 g Sat); 46 mg Cholesterol; 31 g Carbohydrate; 2 g Fibre; 16 g Protein; 1159 mg Sodium

Pictured on page 109.

Variation: Sandwiches can be cooked in ungreased frying pan on medium-hot for 2 to 3 minutes per side.

Domino Brownies

A fudgey brownie with the occasional burst of white chocolate. A fun "domino" look.

Hard margarine (or butter), cut up	1/2 cup	125 mL
Semi-sweet chocolate baking squares (1 oz., 28 g, each), chopped	4	4
Granulated sugar	1/2 cup	125 mL
Large eggs, fork-beaten	2	2
All-purpose flour	1 1/3 cups	325 mL
Salt	1/8 tsp.	0.5 mL
White chocolate baking squares (1 oz., 28 g, each), chopped	3	3
Milk chocolate chips	1/2 cup	125 mL

(continued on next page)

White chocolate baking squares (1 oz., 28 g, each), melted	2	2

Heat margarine and semi-sweet chocolate in medium saucepan on low, stirring often, until chocolate is almost melted. Do not overheat. Remove from heat. Stir until smooth.

Add sugar and eggs. Stir for about 2 minutes until sugar is dissolved.

Add next 4 ingredients. Stir until well combined. Pour into 8 x 8 inch (20 x 20 cm) pan lined with greased foil. Smooth top. Bake in 350°F (175°C) oven for 25 to 30 minutes until set. Do not overcook. Let stand in pan until cooled completely.

Lift brownie onto cutting board. Peel off and discard foil. Cut into 32 pieces (3/4 x 1 1/2 inches, 2 x 3.8 cm, each). Spoon melted white chocolate into small piping bag fitted with small writing tip or into small freezer bag with very small corner snipped from bag. Pipe line across centre of each brownie. Make dots on each end to resemble domino markings. Makes 32 brownies.

1 brownie: 113 Calories; 6.3 g Total Fat (3 g Mono, 0.5 g Poly, 2.5 g Sat); 15 mg Cholesterol; 14 g Carbohydrate; trace Fibre; 2 g Protein; 55 mg Sodium

Pictured below.

Wakey-Wakey!

A delicious way to wake up on the morning after a sleepover. Rouse the kids out of bed with the tempting aromas of these satisfying selections.

serves 6

Raspberry Smoothies

Banana Chip Muffins

Maple Sausage Bites

Spicy Eggburgers

Fruit And Yogurt

Top Left: Banana Chip Muffins, page 116
Top Right: Raspberry Smoothies, page 116
Bottom: Spicy Eggburgers, page 118

Raspberry Smoothies

A sweet, thick shake in a pretty pink shade. Start the kids' day with colour!

Vanilla yogurt	4 cups	1 L
Frozen medium bananas, cut up	2	2
Raspberry jelly preserves	1 cup	250 mL

Process yogurt, banana and jelly in blender, in 2 batches, until smooth. Makes 7 cups (1.75 L). Serves 6.

1 serving: 283 Calories; 3.1 g Total Fat (0.8 g Mono, 0.1 g Poly, 1.9 g Sat); 8 mg Cholesterol; 62 g Carbohydrate; 1 g Fibre; 7 g Protein; 105 mg Sodium

Pictured on page 115.

Banana Chip Muffins

Lightly browned muffins with a delicate banana flavour and lots of chocolate chips—two flavours immensely appealing to most children.

Quick-cooking rolled oats (not instant)	1 cup	250 mL
All-purpose flour	1 cup	250 mL
Whole wheat flour	2/3 cup	150 mL
Brown sugar, packed	1/4 cup	60 mL
Baking powder	2 tsp.	10 mL
Baking soda	1 tsp.	5 mL
Ground cinnamon	1/2 tsp.	2 mL
Salt	1/2 tsp.	2 mL
Mashed banana (about 3)	1 1/2 cups	375 mL
Buttermilk (or reconstituted from powder)	2/3 cup	150 mL
Large egg, fork-beaten	1	1
Cooking oil	1/4 cup	60 mL
Mini semi-sweet chocolate chips	2/3 cup	150 mL

Combine first 8 ingredients in large bowl. Make a well in centre.

Whisk next 4 ingredients together in medium bowl. Add to well.

Add chocolate chips. Stir until just moistened. Divide and spoon into 12 greased muffin cups. Bake in 375°F (190°C) oven for about 20 minutes until wooden pick inserted in centre of muffin comes out clean. Let stand in pan for 5 minutes before removing to wire rack to cool. Makes 12 muffins.

1 muffin: 246 Calories; 9.3 g Total Fat (4.3 g Mono, 1.9 g Poly, 2.5 g Sat); 18 mg Cholesterol; 38 g Carbohydrate; 3 g Fibre; 5 g Protein; 292 mg Sodium

Pictured on page 115.

Maple Sausage Bites

Bites of sausage with a thick, sweet sauce. A delicious breakfast side dish!

Pork breakfast sausages (about 1 lb., 454 g)	12	12
All-purpose flour	2 tsp.	10 mL
Maple (or maple-flavoured) syrup	1/2 cup	125 mL
Lemon juice	1 tsp.	5 mL

Spray large frying pan with cooking spray. Heat pan on medium. Add sausages. Cook for about 15 minutes, turning frequently, until browned and cooked through. Remove to paper towel to drain. Cut into 3 to 4 pieces each. Reserve 2 tsp. (10 mL) drippings in pan.

Reduce heat to low. Add flour to drippings. Stir for about 1 minute until smooth. Slowly add syrup and lemon juice. Heat and stir until boiling. Add sausage. Stir until coated. Serves 6.

1 serving: 168 Calories; 7.3 g Total Fat (3.2 g Mono, 0.9 g Poly, 2.5 g Sat); 29 mg Cholesterol; 21 g Carbohydrate; trace Fibre; 5 g Protein; 278 mg Sodium

Pictured below.

Top and Centre Right: Fruit And Yogurt, page 118   Bottom Left: Maple Sausage Bites, above

Spicy Eggburgers

Chili sauce adds a spicy zip to this breakfast burger. If children prefer, ketchup is a good substitute.

Hard margarine (or butter)	1 tbsp.	15 mL
Large eggs	6	6
Salt, sprinkle		
Pepper, sprinkle		
Grated medium Cheddar cheese	1/3 cup	75 mL
Hamburger buns, split, toasted and buttered	6	6
Chili sauce (or ketchup)	6 tsp.	30 mL
Canadian bacon slices (optional), cooked	6	6

Melt margarine in large frying pan on medium. Add 3 eggs. Prick each yolk with egg shell. Extend yolk almost to edges of egg with pancake lifter. Sprinkle with salt and pepper. Turn over when starting to set.

Sprinkle each egg with 2 to 3 tsp. (10 to 15 mL) cheese. Cover. Heat until cheese melts. Repeat with remaining 3 eggs, salt, pepper and cheese.

Spread each bun with 1 tsp. (5 mL) chili sauce. Add bacon and 1 egg. Makes 6 eggburgers.

1 eggburger: 260 Calories; 12.6 g Total Fat (5.6 g Mono, 1.4 g Poly, 4.3 g Sat); 223 mg Cholesterol; 24 g Carbohydrate; trace Fibre; 12 g Protein; 462 mg Sodium

Pictured on page 115.

Fruit And Yogurt

Serve fresh fruit (such as bananas, cantaloupe, cherries, honeydew, kiwifruit and strawberries) with your child's favourite yogurt for dipping.

Pictured on page 117.

Measurement Tables

Throughout this book measurements are given in Conventional and Metric measure. To compensate for differences between the two measurements due to rounding, a full metric measure is not always used. The cup used is the standard 8 fluid ounce. Temperature is given in degrees Fahrenheit and Celsius. Baking pan measurements are in inches and centimetres as well as quarts and litres. An exact metric conversion is given below as well as the working equivalent (Metric Standard Measure).

Spoons

Conventional Measure	Metric Exact Conversion Millilitre (mL)	Metric Standard Measure Millilitre (mL)
$1/8$ teaspoon (tsp.)	0.6 mL	0.5 mL
$1/4$ teaspoon (tsp.)	1.2 mL	1 mL
$1/2$ teaspoon (tsp.)	2.4 mL	2 mL
1 teaspoon (tsp.)	4.7 mL	5 mL
2 teaspoons (tsp.)	9.4 mL	10 mL
1 tablespoon (tbsp.)	14.2 mL	15 mL

Cups

Conventional Measure	Metric Exact Conversion Millilitre (mL)	Metric Standard Measure Millilitre (mL)
$1/4$ cup (4 tbsp.)	56.8 mL	60 mL
$1/3$ cup ($5^1/3$ tbsp.)	75.6 mL	75 mL
$1/2$ cup (8 tbsp.)	113.7 mL	125 mL
$2/3$ cup ($10^2/3$ tbsp.)	151.2 mL	150 mL
$3/4$ cup (12 tbsp.)	170.5 mL	175 mL
1 cup (16 tbsp.)	227.3 mL	250 mL
$4^1/2$ cups	1022.9 mL	1000 mL (1 L)

Oven Temperatures

Fahrenheit (°F)	Celsius (°C)
175°	80°
200°	95°
225°	110°
250°	120°
275°	140°
300°	150°
325°	160°
350°	175°
375°	190°
400°	205°
425°	220°
450°	230°
475°	240°
500°	260°

Dry Measurements

Conventional Measure Ounces (oz.)	Metric Exact Conversion Grams (g)	Metric Standard Measure Grams (g)
1 oz.	28.3 g	28 g
2 oz.	56.7 g	57 g
3 oz.	85.0 g	85 g
4 oz.	113.4 g	125 g
5 oz.	141.7 g	140 g
6 oz.	170.1 g	170 g
7 oz.	198.4 g	200 g
8 oz.	226.8 g	250 g
16 oz.	453.6 g	500 g
32 oz.	907.2 g	1000 g (1 kg)

Pans

Conventional Inches	Metric Centimetres
8x8 inch	20x20 cm
9x9 inch	22x22 cm
9x13 inch	22x33 cm
10x15 inch	25x38 cm
11x17 inch	28x43 cm
8x2 inch round	20x5 cm
9x2 inch round	22x5 cm
10x$4^1/2$ inch tube	25x11 cm
8x4x3 inch loaf	20x10x7.5 cm
9x5x3 inch loaf	22x12.5x7.5 cm

Casseroles

CANADA & BRITAIN Standard Size Casserole	Exact Metric Measure	UNITED STATES Standard Size Casserole	Exact Metric Measure
1 qt. (5 cups)	1.13 L	1 qt. (4 cups)	900 mL
$1^1/2$ qts. ($7^1/2$ cups)	1.69 L	$1^1/2$ qts. (6 cups)	1.35 L
2 qts. (10 cups)	2.25 L	2 qts. (8 cups)	1.8 L
$2^1/2$ qts. ($12^1/2$ cups)	2.81 L	$2^1/2$ qts. (10 cups)	2.25 L
3 qts. (15 cups)	3.38 L	3 qts. (12 cups)	2.7 L
4 qts. (20 cups)	4.5 L	4 qts. (16 cups)	3.6 L
5 qts. (25 cups)	5.63 L	5 qts. (20 cups)	4.5 L

Recipe Index

Company's Coming cookbooks are available at retail locations throughout Canada!

EXCLUSIVE mail order offer on next page

Buy any 2 cookbooks—choose a 3rd FREE of equal or less value than the lowest price paid.

Original Series — CA$15.99 Canada — US$12.99 USA & International

CODE		CODE		CODE	
SQ	150 Delicious Squares	BB	Breakfasts & Brunches	ASI	Asian Cooking
CA	Casseroles	SC	Slow Cooker Recipes	CB	The Cheese Book
MU	Muffins & More	ODM	One-Dish Meals	RC	The Rookie Cook
SA	Salads	ST	Starters	RHR	Rush-Hour Recipes
AP	Appetizers	SF	Stir-Fry	SW	Sweet Cravings
SS	Soups & Sandwiches	MAM	Make-Ahead Meals	YRG	Year-Round Grilling
CO	Cookies	PB	The Potato Book	GG	Garden Greens
PA	Pasta	CCLFC	Low-Fat Cooking	CHC	Chinese Cooking
BA	Barbecues	CCLFP	Low-Fat Pasta	PK	The Pork Book
PR	Preserves	CFK	Cook For Kids	RL	Recipes For Leftovers
CH	Chicken, Etc.	SCH	Stews, Chilies & Chowders	EB	The Egg Book
KC	Kids Cooking	FD	Fondues	HS	Herbs & Spices **NEW**
CT	Cooking For Two	CCBE	The Beef Book		*August 1/04*

Greatest Hits Series

CODE	CA$12.99 Canada US$9.99 USA & International
ITAL	Italian
MEX	Mexican

Lifestyle Series

CODE	CA$17.99 Canada US$15.99 USA & International
GR	Grilling
DC	Diabetic Cooking

CODE	CA$19.99 Canada US$15.99 USA & International
HC	Heart-Friendly Cooking
DDI	Diabetic Dinners

Most Loved Recipe Collection

CODE	CA$23.99 Canada US$19.99 USA & International
MLA	Most Loved Appetizers
MLMC	Most Loved Main Courses

Special Occasion Series

CODE	CA$20.99 Canada US$19.99 USA & International
GFK	Gifts from the Kitchen
CFS	Cooking for the Seasons

CODE	CA$22.99 Canada US$19.99 USA & International
WC	Weekend Cooking

CODE	CA$25.99 Canada US$22.99 USA & International
HFH	Home for the Holidays
DD	Decadent Desserts
BS	Baking Sensations **NEW** *September 1/04*

COOKBOOKS

COMPANY'S COMING PUBLISHING LIMITED
2311 – 96 Street
Edmonton, Alberta, Canada T6N 1G3
Tel: (780) 450-6223 Fax: (780) 450-1857
www.companyscoming.com

EXCLUSIVE Mail Order Offer
See previous page for list of cookbooks

Buy 2 Get 1 FREE!
Buy any 2 cookbooks—choose a **3rd FREE**
of equal or less value than the lowest price paid.

Quantity	Code	Title	Price Each	Price Total
			$	$

DON'T FORGET
to indicate your
FREE BOOK(S).
(see exclusive mail order
offer above)
please print

	TOTAL BOOKS (including FREE)	TOTAL BOOKS PURCHASED:	$

	International	Canada & USA
Plus Shipping & Handling (per destination)	**$7.00** (one book)	**$5.00** (1-3 books)
Additional Books (including FREE books)	$ ($2.00 each)	$ ($1.00 each)
Sub-Total	$	$
Canadian residents add G.S.T.(7%)		$
TOTAL AMOUNT ENCLOSED	$	$

The Fine Print

- Orders outside Canada must be **PAID IN US FUNDS** by cheque or money order drawn on Canadian or US bank or by credit card.
- Make cheque or money order payable to: **COMPANY'S COMING PUBLISHING LIMITED**.
- Prices are expressed in Canadian dollars for Canada, US dollars for USA & International and are subject to change without prior notice.
- Orders are shipped surface mail. For courier rates, visit our web-site: **companyscoming.com** or contact us:
  Tel: (780) 450-6223 Fax: (780) 450-1857
- Sorry, no C.O.D.

☐ MasterCard. ☐ VISA

_____
Expiry date

Account # _____

Name of cardholder _____

Cardholder's signature _____

Gift Giving

- Let us help you with your gift giving!
- We will send cookbooks directly to the recipients of your choice if you give us their names and addresses.
- Please specify the titles you wish to send to each person.
- If you would like to include your personal note or card, we will be pleased to enclose it with your gift order.

Shipping Address
Send the cookbooks listed above to:

Name: _____

Street: _____

City: _____ Prov./State: _____

Country: _____ Postal Code/Zip: _____

Tel: (   ) _____

E-mail address: _____

☐ YES! Please send a catalogue

New April 1st, 2004

Our most popular main course classics, all in one book! *Most Loved Main Courses* features recipes hand-picked from Company's Coming cookbooks. Discover our recent hits alongside your cherished favourites.

Every recipe is kitchen-tested and beautifully pictured, plus some handy tips we've learned along the way.

Complete your Original Series Collection!

- ❏ 150 Delicious Squares
- ❏ Casseroles
- ❏ Muffins & More
- ❏ Salads
- ❏ Appetizers
- ❏ Soups & Sandwiches
- ❏ Cookies
- ❏ Pasta
- ❏ Barbecues
- ❏ Preserves
- ❏ Chicken, Etc.
- ❏ Kids Cooking
- ❏ Cooking For Two
- ❏ Breakfasts & Brunches
- ❏ Slow Cooker Recipes
- ❏ One-Dish Meals
- ❏ Starters
- ❏ Stir-Fry
- ❏ Make-Ahead Meals
- ❏ The Potato Book
- ❏ Low-Fat Cooking
- ❏ Low-Fat Pasta
- ❏ Cook For Kids
- ❏ Stews, Chilies & Chowders
- ❏ Fondues
- ❏ The Beef Book
- ❏ Asian Cooking
- ❏ The Cheese Book
- ❏ The Rookie Cook
- ❏ Rush-Hour Recipes
- ❏ Sweet Cravings
- ❏ Year-Round Grilling
- ❏ Garden Greens
- ❏ Chinese Cooking
- ❏ The Pork Book
- ❏ Recipes For Leftovers
- ❏ The Egg Book
- ❏ Herbs & Spices **NEW** *August 1/04*

COLLECT ALL
Company's Coming
Series Cookbooks!

Greatest Hits Series
- ❏ Italian
- ❏ Mexican

Lifestyle Series
- ❏ Grilling
- ❏ Diabetic Cooking
- ❏ Heart-Friendly Cooking
- ❏ Diabetic Dinners

Most Loved Recipe Collection
- ❏ Most Loved Appetizers
- ❏ Most Loved Main Courses

Special Occasion Series
- ❏ Gifts from the Kitchen
- ❏ Cooking for the Seasons
- ❏ Home for the Holidays
- ❏ Weekend Cooking
- ❏ Decadent Desserts
- ❏ Baking Sensations
  NEW *September 1/04*

Canada's most popular cookbooks!